The
Birdwatcher's
Year

The Birdwatcher's Year

A Month-by-Month Guide to British Birds

Foreword by
Robin Murrell

Malcolm Greenhalgh

Bounty
BOOKS

First published in Great Britain in 1990 by
Reed Consumer Books Limited

Reprinted in 1993 by Chancellor Press, an imprint of
Bounty Books, a division of Octopus Publishing Group

This edition published in 2013 by Bounty Books,
a division of Octopus Publishing Group Ltd
Endeavour House
189 Shaftesbury Avenue
London WC2H 8JY

www.octopusbooks.co.uk

An Hachette UK Company
www.hachette.co.uk

Copyright © Malcolm Greenhalgh 1990

ISBN: 978-0-753724-43-9

A CIP catalogue record for this book is available from the
British Library

Printed and bound in China

Contents

To the memory of five great ornithologists

Professor Brian Collinge

James Fisher

Maxwell Knight

Sir Peter Scott

Kenneth Williamson

who had a profound influence on a young birdwatcher

Foreword

This is a very exciting and challenging time for environmentalists. Proofs of changes in world climate patterns are needed urgently to persuade politicians that action on the 'greenhouse effect' must be speeded up. Amateur birdwatchers have a vital role to play in this process, because changes in migration patterns and local bird population levels provide us with one of the most sensitive environmental indicators.

Many of us would love to make the transition from casually observing birds to meaningful bird-watching, at a more expert though nonetheless amateur level. I would certainly not describe myself as a birdwatcher, but I have certainly been aware of the differences in species around me as I have moved from one part of the country to another.

Yet it was only recently, when living in suburban Hertfordshire, that the local dominance of green-finches, plus visits to my garden by treecreepers and five varieties of tit, started me thinking about the 'whys' and 'wherefores'. Now that I live in the heart of the Yorkshire Dales National Park, with its three varieties of wagtails, its dippers, hawks, owls and buntings, I realise that I need a bridge to understanding what I see on my daily walks.

Malcolm Greenhalgh's book is just such a bridge: a contribution to better understanding of the world in which we live. *The Birdwatcher's Year* will enable me to derive greater pleasure from the birds I see – and greater knowledge of the environment we share.

Robin Murrell
Editor, *Environment Now*

Introduction

'The study of birds is play. A science often. An art sometimes. But still play.'

James Fisher

Watching birds is one of the greatest of pastimes. To sit amongst the heather by a Hebridean loch and watch a pair of black-throated divers tending their young is a wonderful experience. To be alone on a mountain summit in Scotland with just ptarmigan, dotterels and a singing cock snow bunting for company is incredibly exciting. It really is thrilling to find and identify a lesser yellowlegs on the local sewage farm, a pechora pipit at Spurn Head and a yellow-breasted bunting on Fair Isle. One of the most magical experiences that any birdwatcher can have is to sit, in the twilight of a summer evening, alone on a small rocky islet far out in the Atlantic and have storm petrels and Leach's petrels all around – small, grey, musky-smelling shadows.

However, rarity is not all. The first swallow of spring is always noteworthy, and even though I have been studying wildfowl for 30 years, I still gaze with wonder every time I watch a big skein of pink-feet or a huge ruck of wigeons. The appearance of a siskin or a brambling at the bird-table is enough to disrupt all household affairs, while the evening aerial acrobatics of a cloud of starlings above their roosting quarters is a splendid sight. For me, a heron stalking roach in a shallow mere is as fascinating as a grizzly bear hunting salmon by an Alaskan river. But unfortunately, too often familiarity can breed contempt!

Birdwatching can take several forms. For many, it is simply a matter of noticing what happens to be

Above *Swallows gathering in autumn at Spurn Point in preparation for their long migration to southern Africa.*

Left *Grey heron watched and photographed from a hide on the RSPB reserve at Leighton Moss, Lancashire.*

around in the garden, supplemented with occasional weekend or holiday visits to famous bird reserves. Many birdwatchers are 'twitchers': they are content only when they are chasing after species they have never seen before. Some birdwatchers spend all their free time catching birds, putting rings on their legs and then releasing them in the hope that they will later be recaptured far away, while others specialize in the expensive hobby of bird photography.

Lots of birdwatchers also take part in special surveys, such as the 'Birds of Estuaries Enquiry', the 'National Wildfowl Counts' or the many studies organized by the British Trust for Ornithology (BTO). A few birdwatchers carry out their own special studies of birds that they are particularly interested in, and publish their findings in articles in magazines such as *British Birds* and *Bird Study*, or in books. And a few birdwatchers become professionals, studying major ornithological problems for university zoology departments, the Ministry of Agriculture and the Nature Conservancy. But they all

have one thing in common: the pleasure of birdwatching.

This book is written primarily for the vast majority of birdwatchers, who have either just taken up the hobby or have been content in the past simply to watch whatever flies past. Through reading it, I hope that many will become more active birdwatchers. I hope, too, that this small book will give some insight into the scope of birdwatching and, by looking at what some of our birds are doing during the year, suggest what can be seen, where and when. But I hope that you may consider going further than just *watching*: learn to study what you watch, for then you will see all the more. As in most things in life, the more you put into birdwatching, the more you get out of it. What I have tried to do in this book is suggest ways of putting more into birdwatching so that the rewards will be greater.

Malcolm Greenhalgh
February 1990

The birdwatcher's tools

Binoculars

The most obvious and almost essential piece of birdwatching equipment is a pair of binoculars. However, the variety of binoculars on the market must be quite bewildering for the beginner. How does one choose the right pair?

The first thing to consider is perhaps magnification or, more properly, 'specification'. Binoculars are rated with two numbers separated by a multiplication sign: for instance, 7 × 50, 8 × 30, 25 × 60. The first number is the magnification – in the examples, '7', '8' and '25' respectively. The second number gives the diameter of the objective lens (which is the larger lens at the opposite end to the eye-piece lens). The bigger that lens, the more light can enter the binoculars and thus the brighter is the image. So a pair of 8 × 30 binoculars will tend to give a duller image, especially at dusk, than a pair of 8 × 40 binoculars.

It is also important to remember that, in general, the greater the magnification of the binoculars, the duller will be the image for a given size of objective lens. So a pair of 7 × 50 binoculars gives a much brighter image (though slightly less magnification) than a pair of 10 × 50 binoculars. That is why the Royal Navy provided their officers with 7 × 50 models and referred to them as 'night glasses'.

Greater magnification allows you to see and recognize birds from further away. However, an increase in the degree of magnification generally leads to a corresponding increase in the size of the binoculars: they may be more tiring to use and at the same time more difficult to hold steadily. Also, in general, the more powerful lenses are more difficult and costly to make than lenses of lower magnification. Therefore, you will either have to pay far more for the more powerful binoculars or buy a much cheaper, inferior pair that are the same price as a good-quality pair with a lower magnification.

One other great advantage of binoculars with a lower magnification is that they tend to have a wider field of view and can be focused on birds that are very close. They are therefore much handier for watching birds flitting about in bushes or tree tops, or for spotting birds that are quickly flying past.

On balance, I would suggest that the ideal magnification for a pair of binoculars for the birdwatcher is between '8' and '10', and of specifications in the range 8 × 30, 8 × 40, 8.5 × 44, 10 × 40 and 10 × 50. All have adequate magnification, are convenient to carry and hold still for long periods of time, and give a reasonably bright image.

Counting waders and wildfowl on the Ribble saltmarshes, Lancashire.

A day spent watching gannets as they squabble in their nesting colony is incredibly fascinating, often amusing, and always exciting.

Price is the second, and often a major, criterion in the choice of binoculars. If everyone could afford them then it would be easy to say: 'Go and purchase a pair of Zeiss Dialyt or Leitz Trinovid 10 × 40, for they are the best!' However, I cannot afford them, and neither will the majority of you be able to! Yet it is important to realize that you get what you pay for and that there are no bargain binoculars. Go to a reputable dealer, such as the ones that advertise in the RSPB magazine *Birds*. There you will get better value for money than you will through adverts in news-papers or in your local photographic shops. Try models by Optolith, Mirador, Swift and Zeiss Jena: They are excellent and good value for money.

Telescopes

A lightweight telescope adds greatly to the pleasure of birdwatching, especially when you are watching birds on lakes, estuaries, out at sea or on high cliffs. A mere speck with the naked eye becomes a bird with binoculars, but with a telescope you can identify the bird and watch what it is doing without disturbing it.

For 25 years I have been using a Nickel Supra telescope that has a zoom magnification from × 15–60; I have also tried a range of more modern models. I have found that the ideal magnification for a birdwatcher's telescope is about × 20–30. 'Zoom' telescopes are much more expensive than ones with a fixed magnification so money can be saved by buying one with a magnification set at 20, 25 or 30. Again, buy the best you can afford, through a reputable dealer. It is also worth buying a lightweight tripod so that the telescope is held firmly when you are using it.

With regard to second-hand binoculars and tele-scopes, 'In Focus' of 204 High Street, Barnet, Hert-fordshire EN5 5SZ (telephone 081–449–1445) usually have a good selection of quality second-hand instru-ments available. Good second-hand binoculars and telescopes are far better value for money than cheap, nasty new ones.

Left *A rare wryneck caught for ringing after being watched feeding among sea buckthorn.*

Notebook and pencil

Keeping a birdwatching diary can be extremely useful, besides adding to the pleasure of watching birds. However, it is essential to carry a field notebook and pencil so that your observations can be recorded as they are made. It is all too easy to forget what you have seen when you come to write it up in the evening. A few jottings made on the spot will help enormously.

Record date, time, place and basic weather conditions; then the species you saw, giving special emphasis to unusual ones or particularly large numbers. It is well worth the effort of counting the numbers of, for example, all the waterfowl you see during a trip to a gravel pit and the numbers of golden plovers and lapwings on some fields that you have visited. Keep a record of the numbers of kestrels you see during a long, boring drive down the motorway; keep records of the species that visit your bird-table, your office window or your school playing fields.

One study that I found fascinating, when I was a schoolboy, was the way the numbers of common and black-headed gulls that were feeding at 8.45 am on the rugby pitches varied according to the time of year and weather conditions. It is useful to note such things, and any interesting behavioural features that you may have noticed: for example, displaying mallards, herons gathering twigs for their nests, robins feeding their fledglings on the garden fence. Then, over the years, you will build up a picture of the arrivals and departures of migrants, the behaviour of the commoner species, the way that numbers of birds fluctuate from month to month and year to year, and the occurrence of rarer species. Fascinating stuff, and very exciting when you discover something that nobody else has noticed.

Should you decide to join one of the national surveys organized by the BTO or the Wildfowl Trust, then the notebook will be an essential tool – you will need the field records that it contains to complete the survey forms. Similarly, if you decide to study one place or one species of bird, or to take up 'twitching', then the field notebook will be where you keep your records until you get home and write them up in the permanent diary.

My own diaries go back to 1959, when I was 13 years old. The information that my earlier diaries contain has been useful in providing background data for my later ornithological studies, and I still get pleasure from reading about my first grey phalarope (29 October 1961), Baird's sandpiper (3 October 1963) and my first dipper nest (4 April 1960).

Books and magazines

The pleasure of reading about birds, especially on a cold, wet winter evening, can be almost as great as watching birds. One or preferably two 'Field Guides' are basic necessities for the identification of birds. These, together with the reports of local societies and the literature that is sent to members by the RSPB, Wildfowl Trust and BTO, are essential reading for all birdwatchers.

The bonxie, or great skua, in flight over its Shetland breeding grounds.

If your chief interest is one part of Britain, one special habitat or one group of birds, then you may decide to build up a small library that deals with these. *The Atlas of Breeding Birds in Britain and Ireland*, *The Atlas of Wintering Birds in Britain and Ireland*, *Estuary Birds in Britain and Ireland*, *Birds in Scotland* and *Wild Geese*, published by Poyser, are the sort of books that most birdwatchers in the British Isles would find useful references. Most counties have societies that publish annual bird reports and then, after so many years, a new edition of the 'county bird book'. You can contribute your records (from the diary) to the annual reports. The name and address of your county recorder can be obtained from the BTO (their address is on page 17). Many bird books are very expensive so buy what you can afford and borrow others from the local library. Time spent in background reading is never wasted.

There are also two national magazines: *Bird Watching* (available from newsagents) and *British Birds* (which is available on subscription from Fountains, Park Lane, Blunham, Bedford MK44 3NJ).

Birdwatchers in Scotland can get their own excellent magazine, *Scottish Birds*, from the Scottish Ornithologists' Club, Regent Terrace, Edinburgh.

Clothing
When you are out birdwatching, dress sensibly to blend in with the countryside. Browns and greens are far better than brightly coloured cagoules and tee-shirts. Remember also that our climate can be quite harsh, especially in winter. The duffle coat, though not waterproof, is an ideal garment for winter wear or for long autumn sea-watches. When you go birding on moors and mountains, remember that the weather can change from hot to cold and wet in a matter of minutes – each year many people are caught out and, consequently, suffer from hypothermia. Always take extra clothing (and food) when you go out into the wilds.

Many birdwatchers have adopted the modern lightweight 'trainer' as standard footwear. However, far better are wellies in wet situations and walking boots. I once saw a birdwatcher fall 30 ft down a cliff (fortunately he bounced) and another who slipped on wet grass and smashed his binoculars because they were wearing trainers.

Camera
A camera is not an essential piece of equipment for the birdwatcher, but it is an extremely useful tool. Using a 35 mm SLR camera and a standard lens and a 200 or 250 mm telephoto lens, it is possible to record places and habitats and to obtain 'record' shots of interesting birds. Of course, these will not give the sorts of results that would satisfy a bird photographer, but they will prove that you correctly identified a rare bird far better than words can do. At the end of the year, when most local clubs and societies have 'members' evenings', it provides you with the opportunity of contributing some interesting material for discussion.

Studying birds

For the amateur, there are perhaps two separate sorts of studies that can be easily carried out: a study of the birds in one particular area, or a study of one particular species or family of birds.

Studying the birds in one area through the year is the easiest and most interesting project to start with. However, it is important to choose an area that can be thoroughly covered in one visit: a small gravel pit, a town park, a small area of woodland, a sewage farm, a short length of river valley, an area of shore, a salt-marsh, a patch of moorland, and so on. Visit the area regularly, possibly on Saturday or Sunday afternoons, or evenings in summer. Move slowly and record every species. Try also to count or estimate the numbers of each species on every visit. Besides the diary, you may also construct a chart on which you record the date of the visit and the numbers of the commoner species. You can then look along one line and see how the population of a species has fluctuated through one year. The diary will be a back-up to this chart and will also contain details of weather and notes on interesting behaviour.

During the breeding season, it is worth while drawing a large-scale map of your study area and marking on the map the distribution of breeding territories, using as evidence of territories singing males, nests you may have found, broods you may have seen, and parents carrying food for their chicks. You will be amazed, at the end of the breeding season, how well you have come to know some of the birds that have bred on your patch.

A lot of the information you will gather may be of great use to national surveys. You might fill in 'nest

record cards' for the BTO or offer your study area to the BTO 'common birds census', etc.

A study of one particular species is far more demanding. But it is made easier in some cases because there are small societies (sometimes 'groups' of birdwatchers) who combine their efforts. The Wildfowl Trust co-ordinates much of the work that is being done on waterfowl, the Wader Study Group on waders, and the Seabird Group on sea birds, for instance. Almost certainly someone else will already be studying the bird you want to study. But competitiveness should have no part in birdwatching; and in any case, they will be studying the bird in a different locality so the studies may be quite different in their results. Through membership of our national ornithological societies, you will learn who is studying what you are interested in. Then, through correspondence, telephone calls and perhaps meetings in each other's areas, you can exchange ideas.

The techniques involved in the study of a species can be quite complicated. You may have to find and follow up many nests without increasing the risk of predation by other humans or animals. Or you may

Red kite country. You can watch kites from the roadside here without disturbing them.

A young red-backed shrike, watched and later trapped at Fair Isle Bird Observatory, Shetland.

want to have the birds ringed so that you can identify them individually and also discover aspects of their migrations; this means that you may have to go through the special training necessary before you can obtain a ringing licence.

You may even want to know what your species is eating. In owls and birds of prey this is quite easy, providing you can find a large supply of the pellets that these birds cough up after each meal. The pellets will contain the bones, fur and feathers of their prey. But how do you discover what a flock of lapwings in a field, or treecreepers that are running up tree trunks, are feeding on?

The important thing is to have a go and enjoy it. Too many people sit in front of the television and watch birds doing things on video or film. It is much more exciting in real life!

Identifying and recording rare birds

All birdwatchers enjoy finding and identifying rare birds and then having the record published in local and national bird reports. It is essential, however, to remember that for a record of a rarity to be accepted, full written evidence is always required as to how the bird was identified. It is also important to remember that this information will be required not only for species that are nationally rare, but also for species that are locally rare. For instance, anyone in the British Isles who sees a black kite, a summer tanager or a king eider will need a good description of that bird if the record is to be accepted, for they are national rarities. However, a record of a red kite in Essex, a chough in Yorkshire or a Dartford warbler in Lancashire will require similar details, even though these are not uncommon species in some other parts of the British Isles.

Always carry out the following drill whenever you see a bird that you think may be a rarity:

1. Note its size in relation to other birds that are present.

2. Examine the bird very carefully and note all the outstanding, conspicuous features which cause you to believe that the bird you are looking at is a rare bird and not a common one (for example, call; white wing bars, rump or outer tail feathers; the shape of the wings, bill and tail; the relative length of the legs and bill, etc). It is always worth drawing crude sketches in your field notebook and marking such features on the sketches as they appear to you.

3. Now make a thorough description of the bird, bit by bit, again perhaps using a series of crude sketches as the basis of your notes. Draw the head and note its colours. Draw the body from the side and front, and note down the colours as you see them. Draw outline sketches of the open wing and tail and then, immediately after the bird has made a short flight, mark on the colours of these. Note, too, the colours of the eye, bill, feet and legs.

4. Keep watching the bird and watch how it behaves. Make a note of this.

5. Keep watching. Double check everything that you have noted. Keep watching and recording everything, no matter how trivial it may seem. As the light changes, do certain colours appear to change? If the bird preens and stretches out its wings, describe the shape of the wing: is it pointed or rounded, do the primary feathers stick out like fingers or does the wing have a smooth outline? Never disturb the bird deliberately, but if it flies around describe its flight: are the wing beats fast or slow, does it glide a lot, is its flight in a straight line, zig-zagged or undulating? And so on.

6. Leave quietly and immediately contact some other birdwatchers. Have them come to look at your find. Experienced birdwatchers will make their own notes independently of you: that is important.

7. When you get home, check your identification in your reference books *but alter nothing in your notes*. If you seem to have missed a point, or noted something that ought not to be there, go back the next day if you can and double check with the bird.

8. Write up your notes neatly and send a copy of them, together with a photocopy of your scruffy field notes, to the county recorder (the BTO will provide his or her name and address). Give the names of other observers who might also provide details. Ask the county recorder to send the record on to the *British Birds* Rarities Committee if the record merits it.

The county recording committee and the national *British Birds* Rarities Committee will carefully examine all your notes. They may ask other experts to help them come to a decision. The record will then be either accepted or rejected. If the latter occurs, do not feel too dismayed. Ask them why the record was rejected: they may be able to give you some pointers on difficult identifications that are not mentioned in the books. Remember that most keen birdwatchers have had at least one record rejected, and that we were all disappointed when that happened!

A Manx shearwater, photographed at dead of night on the island of Skomer.

Societies for birdwatchers

The Royal Society for the Protection of Birds,
The Lodge, Sandy, Bedfordshire SG19 2DL

All birdwatchers should be members of the RSPB, and all young people members of the RSPB's junior branch, The Young Ornithologists' Club. No other organization does as much for both birds and birdwatchers.

The Wildfowl Trust,
Slimbridge, Gloucestershire GL2 7BT

All birdwatchers should also be members of the Wildfowl Trust, especially those who enjoy watching waterfowl. The Trust organizes 'National Wildfowl Counts' in winter and they would be pleased to have more volunteers to help with these.

The British Trust for Ornithology,
Beech Grove, Tring, Hertfordshire HP23 5NR

The BTO is the society for the really active birdwatcher. They organize a wide range of national surveys: why don't you join them and take part in some? The BTO is also responsible for the organization of the bird-ringing scheme in the British Isles, so if you want to become a bird-ringer contact them for details of the training programme. The BTO also keeps records of local and county birdwatching societies.

Your County Trust for Nature Conservation.
These are sometimes known as County Naturalists' Trusts: your county will have one and you ought to give them your support.

Your local birdwatching or natural history society.
Join them. You will make lots of friends and have the opportunity of going to evening meetings throughout the winter and on birdwatching excursions during the summer.

Birdwatchers and bird protection

When you are out birdwatching *always* put the welfare of the birds first.

Unfortunately, too many birdwatchers do not. They want to see a bird and they will do anything to see it, no matter what. Almost every year we hear of rare vagrant birds that are literally hounded to death by hordes of selfish 'twitchers'. That is disgraceful. A bird that has arrived in the British Isles after flying continuously for perhaps thousands of miles before making a landfall here is certain to be in a weak state. It should be allowed to feed and build up its strength without being harassed. There have also been incidents when scores of twitchers, intent on seeing a rare bird, no matter what, have invaded private property, broken hedgerows, trampled crops and made a general nuisance of themselves. These thoughtless individuals have also brought birdwatchers, birdwatching and the bird protection movement into disrepute – for the non-birdwatching public do not differentiate between these vandals and the majority.

Each year many birds' nests are destroyed by predators because some birdwatchers wanted a better look and removed the protective cover around the nests. Do not search for birds' nests unless you have a very good reason for doing so. Nest-finding may be essential if you are taking part in a national survey organized by the BTO, or are making your own special study of one area or a species of bird. But do the job carefully, following the advice contained in one of the guides to the subject (*A Field Guide to Birds' Nests* by Bruce Campbell and James Ferguson-Lees is probably the best). If you cannot find the nest

you are looking for within ten minutes, retire and let the birds get on with incubating or feeding their young. When you revisit a nest to check its progress, do so quickly. Always make sure that the vegetation round nests is not disturbed, for predators such as magpies and small boys can become quite adept at following trails of broken nettles to whitethroat nests and battered-down reeds to grebe nests. Be especially careful when looking for the nests of those species that nest on the ground. It is so easy to trample on them. Never disturb a nest that contains young that are close to fledging, for in many cases they will leave the nest prematurely.

In some areas the winter bird flocks, for example of wild geese, are harried so much by birdwatchers that some days they are hardly able to obtain any food. During periods of spring tides, some birdwatchers take great delight in disturbing waders in their roosts at the top of the shore. There are some thickets of dense hawthorn, pine and sea buckthorn that are known to be the roosting sites for long-eared owls, but where the owls are literally kicked out of bed by birdwatchers who would like to see them flying about in the daytime. This is all wrong. There is never any excuse for disturbing birds just so that we can get a better view. If you want to watch birds, be patient and let the birds come confidently to you. This is far better, and often gives better views, than the violent approach.

Far worse, in a way, is the disturbance caused to some of our rare breeding birds by birdwatchers who selfishly get too close. Several species of bird are protected by the Wildlife and Countryside Act, which states that we should not disturb them at or close to their nests (the RSPB produces special notes for its members that you should read carefully). That does not mean that we cannot watch them during the breeding season. Far from it! From roadsides in northern Scotland it is possible to watch divers, Slavonian and black-necked grebes, harriers, eagles, ospreys, greenshanks and other rigorously protected species *without* disturbing them. It is possible to enjoy great views of the Welsh kites without leaving the roads that dissect their territories, and enjoy Savi's warblers and bearded tits without having to batter through reedbeds.

Barnacle geese on Islay in the Inner Hebrides; all these come from Greenland.

One day you might be lucky enough to stumble on a pair of rare birds that are given special protection under the law, which you feel might be nesting where they have never nested before. What you should not do is search for their nest. Instead you should leave immediately and contact the RSPB, either at their headquarters (telephone 0767 680551) or through the warden of the nearest RSPB or Nature Conservancy reserve. They will advise you and, if they think it necessary, join you to investigate.

Sometimes you may see others breaking the law. There are still a few criminals who collect the eggs of rare wild birds. There are still a few misguided gamekeepers who will shoot any bird of prey that flies within gunshot and destroy its nest. There are still some so-called 'sportsmen' who will kill badgers, otters and protected birds. Such barbarians may be quite dangerous. Should you encounter them, note down what they are doing, plus a brief description of them, and car numbers, etc. Then get help from the police and inform the RSPB.

It seems important to stress that in the countryside birdwatchers have no more privileges than groups such as ramblers, and that like them we should follow the Country Code. This means, in England and Wales, that unless there is a public footpath along a river bank, or through a wood, or across a moor, we have no right of access, and that if there is a footpath we have no right to stray from it. I would therefore recommend all birdwatchers who wish to visit regularly any private area of countryside, even if it has a footpath, to visit the owner, farmer, gamekeeper or whoever. They are making their livelihood from the land: we seek just enjoyment. Permission to study the birds of an area is usually given freely. And don't forget that they are there every day, so that they might pass on to you information that they have gathered over many years.

In all birdwatching, let your motto always be: 'The Bird Comes First'.

Right *A young short-eared owl receiving a ring glares at the photographer. Bird ringing is a specialized and skilled technique that requires thorough training.*

Owls in the night

Although January is mid-winter, for three of our resident owls it marks the start of the breeding cycle. Eggs may not be laid until late February or March, but before then there are the tasks of acquiring a territory by the male, of courtship and pairing, of choosing a suitable nest site, and finally the act of mating to be completed. It is therefore usually in January that the males begin the process of gaining a territory. Other males may decide on the same area for their territory, so the male must advertise his presence by calling loudly, which also acts as an invitation to any unmated females to join him.

The commonest and most familiar of our owls is the tawny owl, which occurs in habitats ranging from large urban gardens and town parks to dense conifer plantations and copses at the tree limit of the highest mountains and moorlands. Most know the high-pitched 'tuwhit-too-hooo' call of the male, uttered from dusk onwards, but few can recognize the 'contact' note that is often used by the female in reply: a sharp, thin 'wicka' call.

By contrast, the call of the long-eared owl is less well known, not because the long-eared owl is particularly rare, but because this is the most nocturnal owl and it tends to call very late at night. Long-eared owls usually occur in woodlands that have some mature conifers mixed with the broad-leaved trees, or in pure stands of conifers. They are also more susceptible to disturbance than the tawny owl and so are rarely found in urban or suburban habitats. Thus, a late-night visit to potentially suitable woodland must be specially made to hear the deep 'hooo-hooo' call of the male long-eared owl.

Since they are so nocturnal, long-eared owls are very difficult to watch. By contrast, tawny owls are frequently seen perching on lamp posts, telegraph poles and the gables of houses, or flying silently past at dusk. However, once a calling long-eared owl has been located, it may then be spotted during a visit to the wood during the day. Move quietly through the wood, examining each pine tree carefully; the owl will be asleep, resting on a branch near the trunk.

Barn owls are found in agricultural habitats, particularly where rough meadows, thick hedgerows, and wide, reed-fringed ditches and dykes are abundant. Here they hunt rodents, especially wood mice, short-tailed and water voles, brown rats and common shrews. Such mammals are, of course, rarer in the modern, sterile, 'tidy' farms that have developed over much of Britain in recent decades. But where such farmlands still predominate – for example, in Dumfries and Galloway, the mosslands of north-west England, South Wales, and parts of Devon, Cornwall and Wiltshire – barn owls are still fairly common.

They are the least nocturnal of the three species of owl that we are considering here. They are often seen hunting in mid-afternoon on a winter's day, gliding silently along rough field boundaries or rushy water meadows and dropping quickly to take unsuspecting prey. Many of their man-made nesting sites, in which they also roost by day throughout the year, have been used for generations: old barns (all too many of which have now gone for 'barn-conversion'), the rafters of village churches and the roofs of Victorian village schools. Just as we now call them 'barn' owls, so too were they once called 'church' owls.

From January, when new territories are being selected and mates sought, the barn owl lives up to its other name: the screech owl. The eerie, drawn-out shriek that the birds make in flight is quite spine-chilling when heard for the first time at close quarters, especially when the white ghostly forms are seen gliding past in the half-light.

Three owls that can easily be heard from late winter, but not so easily seen.

LONG-EARED OWL

TAWNY OWL

BARN OWL

Bird-table visitors in winter

Anyone who professes an interest in wild birds and who has even a small garden or backyard ought to have a bird-table and make sure that it is kept well stocked throughout the winter. With a bit of ingenuity it is surprising what a varied list of species can be attracted to the garden.

Grated cheese is loved by robins, while seeds are especially useful, whether bought in a 'wild-bird mix' from the local pet shop or begged from farming friends. These will quickly attract a resident flock of house sparrows, and the house sparrows will in turn attract collared doves, greenfinches, yellowhammers, linnets, reed buntings, chaffinches and tree sparrows. Even moorhens, forced from their usual aquatic haunts by a prolonged freeze, will feast on seeds put out on a suburban lawn.

Woodpeckers and nuthatches are often attracted to feed on the remains of the Christmas turkey or fatty bone from the Sunday roast, hung by a piece of rope from the branch of a tree to deter unwelcome rats and cats. The same species, and also tits, wrens and treecreepers, are fond of fatty foods hidden away in crevices: drill lots of holes in a tree stump and fill them each morning with molten fat, bits of cooked bacon rind, peanuts and old cheese. If a supply of mealworms is available from the pet shop, drop a few of these into some holes in the stump. You can also collect all those bits of food that would normally go into the dustbin: scrapings from dinner plates, fat trimmings from meat, food that has gone stale. Pack these scraps into old yoghurt cartons and pour on cool but still-molten fat from the frying pan – these 'bird puddings' can then be accumulated throughout the year in a corner of the freezer for use in winter. When the time comes to use it, empty the pudding into a plastic mesh-net bag or wire container and hang it up in a tree, where it will attract a wide range of woodland birds.

Thrushes, including blackbirds, song thrushes, mistle thrushes, fieldfares and redwings, are easy to attract into the garden in large numbers with rotting fruit, especially apples or pears. Arrange for the greengrocer to pass on to you those that are no longer fit for sale – he will only throw them away.

Many people buy red plastic mesh bags of peanuts to hang up, or wire containers that they fill with peanuts or food scraps. This is a superb way of attracting several interesting species into the garden but *beware* – buy only the best peanuts. Those that are not fit for human consumption are sometimes harmful to birds as well. Peanuts will attract most of the British tits: blue and great tits most commonly, but also the tiny coal tit. Where the garden is close to large areas of woodland, then marsh or willow tits may join the assemblage. And in the Central Highlands of Scotland, in the Spey Valley, I once had a bird-table that attracted crested tits to the red peanut bag. Two other birds that are very partial to seeds and peanuts are the brambling and siskin.

It is also worth considering including some special plants in the garden that will provide food in winter for the birds, such as sunflowers (for seeds) and berry-bearing bushes – pyracantha and cotoneaster are perhaps the best, but rowan is also very good. But be sure to cover some with bird-proof netting in the autumn or else the local blackbirds will strip them before the winter. Then, each week, uncover a few more berry-laden branches. Besides thrushes, you may also succeed in attracting the rare waxwing, a very special winter visitor from Siberia that feeds mainly on berries in winter. In 1973 a tiny garden in the middle of Southport had redwings and waxwings feeding on pyracantha berries.

COAL TIT

BRAMBLING

SISKIN

It is surprising what can be attracted to a bird-table in winter, even in the most urban garden or backyard. We can all enjoy the sight of bramblings, siskins and coal tits feeding on peanuts in red holders.

Three winter geese

Of the seven species of geese to be found in the British Isles in winter, four are widespread in their distribution: the greylag, pink-foot, brent and (feral) Canada goose. The other three are much more localized: the white-front, barnacle and bean goose.

Two distinct forms of the white-fronted goose visit the British Isles in winter. Those that breed in Greenland winter mostly on the vast peat bogs and coast of Ireland, with the biggest concentration of over 6000 on Wexford Slobs. About 5000 also winter in the Hebrides (notably on Islay), with smaller gaggles by Loch Ken (Dumfries and Galloway) and the Dovey estuary in Wales. Greenland white-fronts are readily recognized by their orange bills and, in the adults, very heavy dark barring on the belly. By contrast, the European white-fronted goose, which breeds in Siberia, has a pink bill and is less heavily barred on its underparts. This form of the white-front winters mostly in the Low Countries of mainland Europe, with just a few regular flocks visiting Britain, the best known being the flock of about 4000 that visits the Wildfowl Trust headquarters at the New Grounds in Gloucestershire.

The barnacle geese that winter in the British Isles also comprise two distinct populations, but they cannot be distinguished from each other by sight. All of the barnacle geese that breed in Greenland winter around the Irish coast or in the Hebrides, most of them (about 20,000) on Islay. By contrast, all of the barnacle geese that breed on the Arctic islands of Svalbard, to the north of Norway's North Cape, winter on the Solway Firth. Most of these, totalling up to 12,000, can be seen on the Wildfowl Trust sanctuary and National Nature Reserve at Caerlaverock (Dumfries and Galloway).

The bean goose is by far the rarest of these three geese, though up to the end of the 19th century it was probably more abundant than the now-common greylag and pink-foot. Drainage of its wet-meadow, rushy-pasture and freshwater-marsh feeding areas in Britain possibly contributed to the decline, though some ornithologists blame the desertion of breeding grounds in Scandinavia. Only two small regular flocks remain in Britain: up to about 300 in the Yare Valley in Norfolk, and less than 100 in the Carron Valley in Scotland.

Unlike the greylag and pink-foot, which feed to a large extent on stubbles, old potato fields, overwintering winter wheat and barley and other arable crops, and the brent goose which feeds on marine plants, these three species of geese are predominantly grazers on natural grasslands. Barnacle geese and European white-fronts frequent coastal pastures and grassy salt-marshes. Greenland white-fronts will also feed on pastures, though their main food appears to be the shoots, rhizomes and bulbils of sedges and cotton-grass on peat bogs. Bean geese also take the shoots and seeds of semi-aquatic bog plants as well as grasses on water meadows. Like all wild geese, they are very faithful to their wintering grounds and may stay and suffer rather than find pastures new.

The Svalbard barnacle geese, which winter on the Solway, are a case in point. During the 19th century this population was estimated at over 10,000. Then, through the first half of the 20th century, numbers crashed. By 1948, only 300 remained. Uncontrolled wildfowling on the Solway was partly to blame, while on the Arctic breeding grounds many eggs were eaten by the Norwegian mining community. However, in 1972 the main breeding areas were given sanctuary status by the Norwegian government. The birds responded, and by 1980 the population had recovered to its 19th-century level.

Wild geese are spectacular, especially when they occur in huge flocks. It is also interesting to learn to identify the various species that winter in the British Isles.

BARNACLE GOOSE

WHITE-FRONTED GOOSE

BEAN GOOSE

Bird of the month: Dartford warbler

The Dartford warbler is one of three species of birds that take their name from the county of Kent but no longer breed there, the others being the Sandwich tern and the Kentish plover. It is the only species of warbler that is resident throughout the year in the British Isles, with the exception of the rare Cetti's warbler, which has colonized Britain in recent years.

Dartford warblers are extremely selective in their choice of habitat, occurring in lowland heath and heath scrub in southern England. The typical territory is dominated by old lanky heather, up to 3 ft high, with plenty of gorse bushes and a few scattered trees. Given time, such habitats progress to woodland, so they must be maintained by grazing or periodic burning, which destroys any young trees. One major problem has been that these heaths are very unproductive from an agricultural point of view, and in the 19th and 20th centuries large areas of heath were destroyed and the land turned over to pasture or arable production, or they were turned over to high-density pine plantations. So only a tiny fraction of these lowland heaths remains today – some of the best areas thankfully preserved as nature reserves – and through the last 150 years there has been a corresponding decline in the numbers of Dartford warblers and a great contraction of their range.

In the 19th century, breeding was recorded in most southern English counties, from Cornwall east to Kent, and north through Essex to Suffolk on the east coast and to Hertfordshire, Oxfordshire, Shropshire and, possibly, Staffordshire in the Midlands. Today, Dartford warblers are restricted to east Devon, Dorset, Hampshire, Sussex, Surrey and the Isle of Wight, with the majority of them found on the heaths of Dorset and Hampshire.

Like all warblers, this species is insectivorous, feeding on insects and spiders. In even the mildest of winters such foods are sparse, but in hard winters with heavy snowfalls it is very difficult for the birds to obtain sufficient quantities to sustain them. In severe winters, therefore, the population of Dartford warblers is usually hard hit, falling dangerously low.

Should a further loss of the Dartford warbler's heathland habitat occur, either by reclamation or through uncontrolled summer fires that can destroy an entire heath, then the population might be reduced to a point where it is either wiped out or is brought to a low level from which it cannot recover following future hard winters. If our population were to become extinct, then there seems no chance of it being replaced by birds colonizing from further south, for the British population is completely isolated from the populations in the Channel Islands and mainland Europe. It is essential, not only for the future of the Dartford warbler, but also for several other plants and animals (such as the rare sand lizard and smooth snake) which are restricted to this special habitat, that all the remaining heathlands of southern England be preserved and managed as nature reserves.

The Dartford warbler is a very secretive species which spends the day skulking in the dense gorse and heather and rarely flies more than a few yards from one patch of cover to the next. It is best located by its characteristic, metallic 'tchurr' or its short, hard 'tuk' calls. Then it is a matter of waiting and watching for the bird to appear briefly. Bright, sunny winter days are perhaps as good a time as any to watch Dartford warblers, for they often occur in small parties which range widely across the heath in search of food. However, great care should be taken when these birds are nesting during spring and summer to avoid disturbing them.

Once a widespread species through southern England, the Dartford warbler has become quite rare because of man's destruction of its heathland habitat.

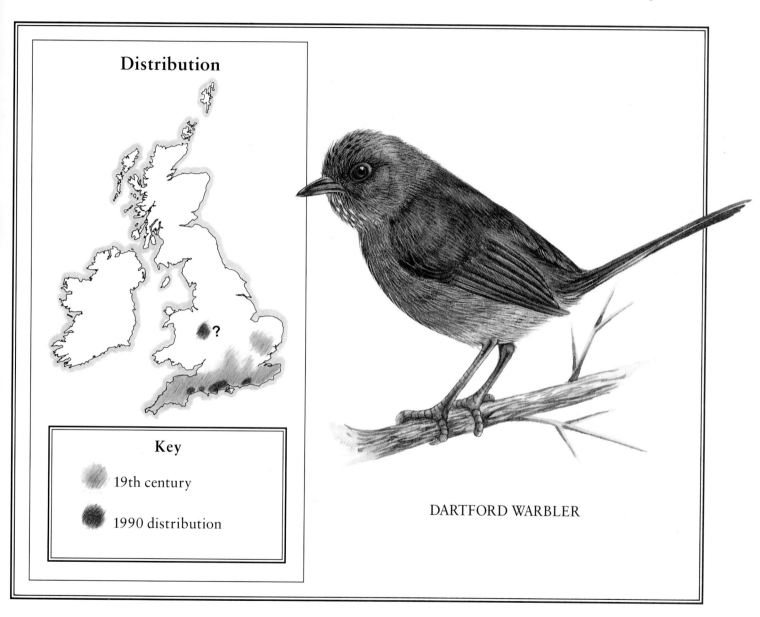

Distribution

Key

19th century

1990 distribution

DARTFORD WARBLER

Hard-weather movements

It is perhaps in January more than in any other month that hard winter weather occurs in the British Isles. In most years, periods of sub-zero temperatures or heavy snowfall may last for only a few days; but in others, notably 1947 and 1963, arctic conditions may prevail for many weeks without respite. Most species of birds can withstand short periods of harsh weather by utilizing the thick fat deposits that are laid down under the skin and around the inner organs, but few can survive prolonged winter conditions. Waterside birds suffer most because their food supplies are hidden beneath a thick layer of ice: in the winter of 1963 the populations of herons and kingfishers were decimated over much of the British Isles, and it took several years before their numbers had risen to the pre-1963 levels. Many other resident species also suffer, not just because of the scarcity of food but more often because they cannot find drinking water. In the same winter of 1963, huge numbers of thrushes and wrens died, not so much from the intense cold and lack of food, but from dehydration. Those of us who put out food for the birds in winter should bear this in mind by providing water as well as food, and by changing the water as soon as it freezes.

Many species of birds try to avoid harsh winter weather by seeking a milder climate as soon as the snow or frost arrives. These movements, known as hard-weather movements, are quite often conspicuous. In winter, large flocks of lapwings and golden plovers, together with smaller numbers of snipe and jack snipe, frequent most areas of damp low-lying meadow and pasture where they feed on insect larvae and earthworms living in the top few centimetres of the soil. With the advent of snow or when the ground freezes, these food organisms burrow deeper and the birds are unable to probe the soil for them. So, with the onset of hard weather, these birds depart. Where one mild January day a field may have held over 1000 birds, the next day there are none. Throughout the first one or two days of freezing weather, flocks of lapwings and golden plovers can be seen flying overhead on a south-westerly track, and the stillness of the icy night air may be punctuated by the 'scape' note of snipe that are also fleeing westwards. When eastern and northern Britain is ice-bound but the milder west is still open, huge congregations descend on the coastal farmlands of Lancashire, Cheshire, West Wales and Cornwall. When these, too, are in the grip of ice and snow, the flocks will travel across the Irish Sea where western Ireland, kept ice-free by mild Atlantic winds, offers sanctuary. Should the freeze also include Ireland, then the birds may continue their travels to the Iberian Peninsula and the Mediterranean.

When the countries that border the Baltic become affected by snow and ice, many species of birds make hard-weather movements to Britain. This often involves huge numbers of waterfowl. Most of the pale-bellied brent geese that breed in Spitsbergen spend the winter in Denmark, but a few also cross the North Sea to winter on the oozy tidal flats of Lindisfarne in Northumberland. In a mild winter the Lindisfarne flock may number less than 100 birds, but with the onset of harsh winter weather in eastern Europe the rest of the population may be forced to quit Denmark and join the Lindisfarne birds. One day there may be just 40 or 50 brents grazing the eel-grass of Fenham Flats; the next day there may be up to 3000 there. With these brents may be many extra thousands of wigeons, whilst on Holy Island there may be scores of woodcocks that have sought the mild weather of the British coast. The weather reports from the Baltic confirm that these are 'hard-weather migrants'.

Right *Lapwings and golden plovers heading southwest in the first snowfall of winter. As soon as a spell of hard weather occurs, watch out, and at night listen, for flocks of birds fleeing the country.*

Woodland birds
in winter

Woodlands are often quite silent places in winter and may seem at first sight almost birdless. Of course, there are exceptions, notably the pheasant covert where the gamekeeper makes a twice-daily round to scatter grain for his birds (see also page 114). He has four good reasons for doing this. Firstly, during the shooting season he can make a quick count so that he can be sure of the sport the following Saturday. Then, he also will know that the pheasants are well fed and in good condition. And, most importantly, he will be certain that his birds do not stray on to his neighbour's land and provide free sport for someone else! Then, after the shooting season is over, in February, he can entice the remaining birds into areas where they can be caught and taken into breeding pens. As he walks down the rides, scattering the grain and uttering a thin sharp whistle, the pheasants come running from the cover on either side. But just as the pheasants associate the whistle with food, so too do the wild birds. Sparrows, finches and tits also join in.

However, in woodlands where extra food is not put out for the birds, the wild foods quickly become exhausted, so that by late winter little remains. A solitary blackbird breaks the silence as it rummages through the rustling fallen leaves for a morsel; in a month's time this wood will have 12 pairs of nesting blackbirds. But where are they all now? Where, too, are the nuthatches, treecreepers and woodpeckers? They are unseen and unheard.

One of the problems is that many of the birds that will be nesting in the wood in the coming spring *are* there. The difficulty is that they have not yet settled in territories and in many cases wander freely from wood to wood, and from woodland to other habitats such as farmlands and gardens in search of food. However, in a large area of woodland a slow, silent approach will usually reveal far more than a cursory glance. There may, for instance, be just one roaming flock of small birds foraging through the tree tops. Overlook them and you will have overlooked blue, great, coal and marsh tits, goldcrests, and perhaps treecreepers, redpolls and siskins.

Three of the most conspicuous birds in woodlands in late winter are the woodpigeon, robin and wren. No one should overlook them! February sees a great increase of woodpigeons as flocks of visitors from Scandinavia swell the numbers of resident birds. Woodpigeons feed mainly on arable land, stripping the leaves from winter cabbages and sprouts, grazing the clover from leys, thinning out the winter cereal crops and playing havoc with newly-sown seeds. Most of their foods are very bulky and require some time for digestion, so between meals the wood-pigeons flight to nearby woodlands to rest. The 'clap-clap' of their wings as they are disturbed from the tree-tops is a characteristic woodland noise, especially in February.

Both the wren and robin are likely to be heard singing now, for these are two species that continue to sing through most of the year and reach fortissimo in late winter and early spring. Incidentally, the robin is one songbird that maintains a territory throughout the winter, which it advertises with song and defends against other robins. Both the male and female have separate winter territories and will not tolerate each other's presence before nesting time. Thus, the female robin proclaims her winter territory like the male, with song, and should the male trespass into her territory she will vigorously attack him. Wrens and woodland robins (unlike our tame garden robins) are quite skulking birds. When disturbed, they will seek dense cover and scold the intruder, whether stoat, fox or man, with a sharp 'tic-tic' note.

ROBIN

WREN

WOODPIGEON

Woodlands can appear almost birdless in mid-winter, when woodpigeons, wrens and robins are among the most conspicuous species.

Winter on the mountain tops

The summits of Scotland's highest mountains are dangerous places in winter. Except in the mildest of winters, they are locked in snow from November to May. At 4000 ft on the Cairngorms, I have known snow to fall in July and sleet in August! At such altitudes, conditions are arctic. But a trek over these highlands on a sunny day in late winter can reveal some ornithological highlights that are easily overlooked in summer, even though many of the summer birds are missing. The dotterels, wheatears and ring ouzels are in Africa but will return at the end of their long spring migrations; the meadow pipits, dunlins and golden plovers are in their winter habitats by the coast. Only the hardiest of upland birds remain.

However, for many of those birds that have overwintered on the hills, the breeding season has already started by the end of February. This is most noticeable on the lower heather slopes where the red grouse are displaying. The cock red grouse takes up its territory in autumn, but it is not until February that it grows pugnacious enough to chase away all intruders but its mate. Those that fail to obtain a territory are driven from the moor by the territory holders; some may be able to gain a territory on an adjacent moor should there be one vacant, but the majority just disappear and presumably die. This is nature's way of ensuring the survival of the red grouse. A territory is just large enough to enable a pair of grouse to raise their brood. Only the fittest grouse can gain a territory and breed; surplus individuals are sacrificed for the benefit of the species. So in February the moor is alive with the calls of displaying cock grouse, a croaking 'ka-ka-ka-ka' followed by a low-pitched 'kowa-kowa-kowa', and squabbles as intruders are chased off.

Golden eagles are in the later stages of preparation for nesting in February. Most pairs have two or three nests within their territory. Some pairs use them on a two- or three-year rotation whereas others change nest only after one has been disturbed during the previous breeding season. On mild days throughout the winter, the pair may have visited all the eyries in their territory and perhaps added a sprig of heather or a clump of woodrush. But in February, visits are more frequent to the eyrie that will be used in the coming spring and summer. The nest is built up, a lining is added of soft rushes or sheep's wool, and the pair may mate on or close to the chosen nest. With all this activity, together with the routine of catching the day's food (they may not have fed for several days if the visit follows a spell of bad weather), February offers superb opportunities for watching golden eagles. It is perhaps the best time to watch them, from a vantage point high on the hill, hunting grouse or mountain hares on the lower slopes.

The only two other birds that can be guaranteed on the mountain in February are the raven and hooded crow. The latter is especially interesting for it was once thought to be a separate species from southern Britain's carrion crow. We now know that they are colour 'morphs' of the same species. The hoodie occurs throughout Ireland, the Isle of Man, and Scotland north and west of a line from Glasgow to Banff. Elsewhere, the carrion crow occurs and the hoodie does not. And along this boundary is a zone where the two forms readily interbreed: a hybrid zone where half hooded and half carrion crows may be seen. On a clear February day both the raven and hooded crow will be preparing for breeding. For although winter may last for several more weeks on the high moors, this month marks the beginning of the nesting season for the resident upland birds.

HOODED CROW

GOLDEN EAGLE

♀

PTARMIGAN

♂

Few birds can withstand the severe winter conditions of the mountains of northern Scotland. But ptarmigan will remain on the highest plateaux and golden eagles and hooded crows will scout the high corries and moorland slopes in search of food.

Winter gulls

Throughout the British Isles gulls are more conspicuous in the winter months than they are during the spring and summer, when they are nesting. And from autumn through to spring, several quite rare species of gull can be found among the flocks of commoner species.

Possibly the most misnamed of British gulls is the 'common' gull, for as a breeding species it is very local in its distribution and quite uncommon in many regions in the summer. Common gulls nest quite rarely in lowland Britain. To find their nests one usually has to visit Scotland or north-western Ireland, where they breed on remote boggy moors, by lochs and on coastal dunes, shingle and marshland. However, in autumn this population spreads out through the British Isles and is joined by many thousands from mainland Europe. Their chief feeding habitat is grassland, where they join with black-headed gulls to probe the turf surface for earthworms, slugs and insect larvae. They seem especially fond of school playing fields, where the work put in by the groundsmen to improve the turf often results in very high densities of earthworms. And the timing of their arrival and departure on the lowland playing fields often matches term times: common gulls generally appear in early September and depart about the beginning of the Easter holiday!

Only two species of gull are truly winter visitors to the British Isles: the Iceland and glaucous gulls. Again, the name 'Iceland' gull is incorrect, for the Iceland gull does not nest in Iceland, its nearest breeding stations being in Greenland! The glaucous gull, which does breed in Iceland, is the larger of the two, being about the size of a great black-backed gull whereas the Iceland is roughly the size of the herring gull. This feature, and the fact that the Iceland gull has a slighter build and wings that, at rest, stick out far beyond the tail, is the way to separate the two species in the field. They are very similar in plumage colouration, immature birds being a pale creamy buff, adults a pale version of a herring gull, and in all plumages the flight feathers are distinctly white rather than the black found in our commoner species.

Glaucous gulls generally outnumber Iceland gulls in Britain by between 10:1 and 20:1. Quite large numbers are sometimes recorded in the fishing harbours of northern Scotland, such as Stornoway, Kinlochbervie, Ullapool and Scrabster. Further south they are scarcer. But wherever there are large congregations of the commoner gulls, then, in winter, at least one glaucous and possibly an Iceland gull will appear. Rubbish tips, evening roosts on reservoirs, estuary mudflats, fishing harbours: all are good places to find these scarce winter gulls.

The little gull is another species that is a visitor to the British Isles. During the last 30 years the numbers appear to have increased tremendously, and in the last ten years or so a few pairs have remained to nest. February sees the arrival of the first large flocks, consisting mostly of adult birds returning on migration to nesting grounds in Europe. Later, in May parties of immature birds may stay for several days. Then, through the autumn, from late July, there is the return migration of adults and juvenile birds which stay in the British Isles for a few weeks before continuing their migration to winter quarters in the Bay of Biscay and the Mediterranean.

Little gulls are delightful birds to watch, being far more graceful than the clumsier, larger species, especially when they are feeding in flight on tiny items of food lying on the water's surface. And their range of winter/summer and adult/immature plumages adds an extra dimension that is well worth noting.

LITTLE GULL

COMMON GULL

GLAUCOUS GULL

Gulls provide the birdwatcher with a variety of identification problems. Check carefully every gull you see, for among the commoner species you will often find the rarer ones.

Bird of the month: Brent goose

Three quite discrete populations of brent geese visit the British Isles in winter. By far the most abundant is the population that breeds in Arctic Siberia and winters on the coasts of England as well as the shores of the Low Countries and France. These birds can be distinguished from the other two populations by their very dark undersides; thus they are known as dark-bellied brents.

The other populations, which cannot be separated from each other in the field, have almost white underparts and are referred to as pale-bellied brents. One population of pale-bellied brents breeds in Greenland and winters around the coast of Ireland. The other population breeds on the Arctic island group of Svalbard and winters in northern Denmark and in the Lindisfarne area of Northumberland.

In winter, brent geese feed predominantly on muddy shores where their main diet comprises eel-grass (or *Zostera*), together with lesser amounts of marine algae such as *Enteromorpha*. During the first half of the 20th century the stocks of eel-grass were decimated by a viral infection and the brent goose populations crashed. From about 70,000 dark-bellied brents in the whole of Europe in 1930, only 16,500 remained in 1955–56. At Lindisfarne, where at least 10,000 pale-bellied brents visited at the end of the 19th century, only five were reported in 1939.

During the 1950s, the brent goose was given legal protection in Britain and in some of its mainland European winter quarters. At the same time, the eel-grass started to make a recovery and the geese also began to turn more to feeding on coastal grasslands. Slowly almost all the populations increased.

Today, about 100,000 dark-bellied brents winter in England, most of them in the bays, harbours and estuaries of Norfolk, Hampshire, Sussex and Essex. The Wash and Foulness regularly support over 20,000, the Blackwater estuary in East Anglia and Chichester harbour on the south coast over 10,000. And smaller, but still sizeable, flocks occur wherever there is suitable tidal muddy habitat along the coast from the Humber to Devon. Brents can be seen feeding even in the middle of London on the Thames mudflats. The Irish pale-bellied brents have similarly increased to over 24,000, the majority of which occur in Strangford Lough (Co. Down) and Lough Foyle (Co. Londonderry).

The number of the Svalbard population of pale-bellied brents that visit Lindisfarne seems to depend, to some extent, on the weather (see page 28). This was first noted by the Victorian wildfowler and naturalist Abel Chapman, who had a punt-gun permanently in readiness at his Holy Island wildfowling headquarters for the arrival of the 'big battalions'! When the weather remains mild in the Danish wintering grounds, only small numbers of brents, possibly only 300 or so, will cross the North Sea to Lindisfarne. However, should harsh icy or snowy weather take its grip of Denmark, then the entire population – which currently numbers about 3000 – will make the crossing.

The British Isles has a greater variety of wild geese than any comparable area of the world: greylag, pink-feet, white-front, bean, barnacle and brent. For several populations of geese, the British Isles provide their sole wintering areas. The total number of wild geese that visit the British Isles in winter is huge compared with numbers in many other parts of the world – about half a million. Yet ours is a small, densely-populated group of islands. It is therefore essential that estuaries, bays, harbours, marshes and inland habitats, which these geese rely on for their winter survival, are carefully conserved.

The brent goose is one of the most fascinating of our winter geese. There are three separate populations to look out for. It is our only truly marine goose, and the fluctuation in its numbers over the last century is remarkable.

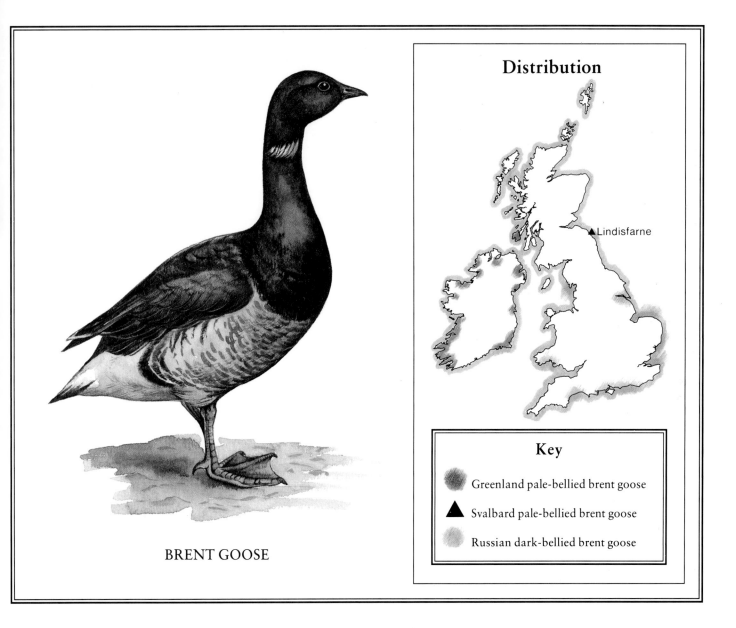

Distribution

▲Lindisfarne

Key

Greenland pale-bellied brent goose

▲ Svalbard pale-bellied brent goose

Russian dark-bellied brent goose

BRENT GOOSE

Winter habitats

It is interesting how many species of birds that remain in the British Isles through the year have a summer breeding habitat and a different winter habitat. We often consider the golden plover and curlew to be moorland birds for that is where they breed. However, they spend less than half the year on the uplands and more than half in their winter habitats: tidal mudflats and low-lying wet pastures. In northern Britain, many pairs of oystercatchers nest in river valleys and feed their young on earthworms and insects collected from riverside meadows. The same oystercatchers then spend the winter on the shore, feeding on mussels and cockles. Reed buntings nest mostly in stands of reeds and rushes by ponds, lakes and rivers, where they feed their young on insects and soft seeds. In autumn, the winter seed diet in this habitat becomes quickly depleted so most reed buntings move to winter habitats, roaming salt-marshes, farmland stubbles and even gardens in search of a seed supply. In winter, our gardens also attract species like the coal tit, greater spotted woodpecker and treecreeper, birds that are specialist woodland birds in summer. And a woodland spar-rowhawk may on occasion visit our bird-table to feed on the birds that are feeding on the food we have put out for them.

Some species of aquatic birds make similar changes, none more so than the divers and grebes. Two species of divers breed in the British Isles: the black-throated diver nests on large freshwater lochs in the north-west of Scotland and the red-throated diver on smaller lochans, often the tiniest of pools, in Scotland and north-west Ireland. The black-throat feeds in its breeding loch on small freshwater fish whereas the red-throat usually flies out to sea to feed on small marine fish. But once the breeding season is over, these divers head for their winter habitat, the shallow inshore seas around the entire coast of the British Isles.

Great crested grebes are common nesting birds on the lakes, gravel pits and reservoirs of lowland England, Scotland and Ireland. Little grebes are even more widespread, breeding in the reedy margins of large lakes and by the smallest of ponds and narrow-est of canals and rivers. Much rarer are the Slavonian grebe, which breeds on a few lochs in northern Scotland, and the black-necked grebe, of which up to about 20 pairs breed on weedy pools scattered across the British Isles. However, as soon as their young can fly strongly, usually in late August or September, all the Slavonian and black-necked grebes and many of the great crested grebes leave their freshwater sum-mer habitat and go to sea for the winter. Little grebes and some great crested grebes remain on freshwater, but should there be a prolonged freeze that ices over their freshwaters, then these will also move on to salt-water for survival. So too must other freshwater birds – those that will not move away, such as the heron and kingfisher, are the ones that suffer greatest and have the highest mortality in prolonged periods of freezing weather.

Coastal habitats certainly provide the richest feeding for so many birds that they are major winter habitats. The sea and estuaries rarely freeze, so they can accommodate water birds, while the intertidal mud and sand-flats are bathed twice each day by the relatively warm sea. The saltmarshes, dunes and low-lying coastal farmlands, too, are influenced by the sea and the warm onshore winds, so compared with inland habitats they rarely freeze and are seldom covered with snow for long periods. Thus, when many inland sites are almost birdless, these winter habitats contain large numbers of several species.

Right *A hen harrier hovers above a brace of snipe concealed in a reedbed, with curlews, redshanks and a flock of dunlins in the background. In winter many birds leave their inland summer habitats and seek coastal habitats where conditions are often milder and food far more plentiful.*

The start of the breeding season

Though some birds begin breeding as early as late January and February, especially in mild winters, many of our resident birds do not begin until March, and some wait until April or even May.

The rook is traditionally one of the earliest of nesters. It is also one of our most conspicuous nesting birds, partly because it builds such large nests in the early season before the trees are in leaf, and partly because it is a colonial breeder in rookeries that may contain upwards of 100 nests. Often as early as late December some older birds are back, refurbishing their nests. Activity increases through January and February as rooks that are going to breed for the first time display, pair, and build nests. By the middle of March, most birds have laid their eggs and incubation is well under way.

The mistle thrush is sometimes called the 'storm-cock' because the males begin singing so early in the year in quite wintry weather. By early February they usually have territories, and by the middle of that month some have begun to construct nests. Although the usual site for their bulky nest is a fork in a branch high in a tree, many nest in town and city centres on buildings. By the end of March, many mistle thrushes are feeding newly-hatched young.

Many water birds also begin nesting before winter is truly over. Herons and mallards may be incubating their eggs before the end of February. During late January and early February, several other species prepare for breeding by obtaining a territory and pairing. For instance, the little grebe or dabchick begins making its high-pitched, trilling, whinnying 'song' from mid-January, signifying that the breeding season is nigh; and by February they are paired and on their territories. Should a spell of hard weather freeze the lake, the grebes will move away to open water elsewhere. But as soon as the ice thaws, they rapidly return and resume where they left off. By the end of February, most dabchicks have started to construct their nests, a simple floating mound of rotting waterweed that is anchored to rushes or willow shoots close to the water's edge. By the end of March, most dabchicks are sitting on a clutch of eggs that slowly turn from white to dirty brown as they become stained by the sodden nest material.

Why do so many birds start nesting so early in the year when the weather can be so foul? Would it not be better for them to start later in the spring? The answer is that they must start early if they are to raise their young to a level of independence that enables them to survive the following winter. Although the young rooks, produced by eggs laid in March, will leave the nest in June, for many weeks after this they are dependent on their parents to provide them with the majority of their food while they are learning to feed for themselves. It is essential that they have this 'learning time' before winter sets in, otherwise they would starve.

There is another side to it, though. By starting the breeding season very early in the year, the young leave the nest at a time when food is most abundant. So, the young from the earliest mistle thrush clutches fledge in mid to late April when the populations of earthworms, slugs and insect larvae in the soil are active. The first broods of dabchicks hatch and immediately leave the nest in April when the water temperature is beginning to rise and their aquatic invertebrate foods are increasing.

That is also why most birds stop breeding in mid-summer. They might have time to lay another clutch of eggs and raise another brood to fledging, but the chances of those young surviving the winter would be almost nil.

ROOK

MISTLE THRUSH

LITTLE GREBE

Several species of bird begin nesting before winter is truly over, among them the rook, mistle thrush and little grebe, or dabchick.

A coastal migration in late winter

Several species of birds that breed on freshwater spend the winter on salt water. The problem is that their breeding lakes in northern Europe, including the British Isles, are quite likely to freeze over for at least part of the winter. Also, the small freshwater fish and invertebrates on which they feed tend to be less accessible in the winter because they are either hibernating or hiding away in mud, amongst boulders and in weedbeds.

The inshore waters around the British Isles very rarely freeze, and the populations of small fish and crustaceans in some of the bays and estuaries are huge. Thus, they make ideal winter quarters (see page 38). For instance: large numbers of divers, grebes and ducks that are freshwater birds in summer but marine birds in winter occur on the shallow waters of Lindisfarne, the Scottish Firths, and Morecambe and Liverpool Bays. Red-throated divers, great crested grebes and wildfowl such as the red-breasted merganser, scaup, goldeneye, long-tailed duck and common and velvet scoters are the most common and widespread. However, there are usually numbers of less common species with them.

The numbers of many of these species often reach a peak during February and early March. There are two reasons for this. Firstly, it is in late winter when the greatest number of lakes in northern Europe are iced up, forcing any birds that have tried to stay on freshwaters to move out. It is not unusual, for instance, for lakes in Britain to be ice-free until late January or February, and then for an extremely severe spell to cause them to ice over. In this way, many hundreds of great crested grebes are displaced to coastal waters.

However, as daylength increases in late winter, so it triggers off the production of reproductive hormones in most birds. Slowly the birds approach breeding condition and, in some cases such as the divers and grebes, begin to moult. The drab grey-and-white winter plumage of the divers and grebes is replaced by the more strikingly-marked breeding plumage. At the same time, the birds begin to move northwards, towards their breeding grounds.

This movement is slow but, judging from counts made at several sites around the British coast, quite distinct. Through February, large numbers of red-throated, black-throated and great northern divers pass northwards through the North Sea and Irish Sea. By March, flocks totalling several hundreds can be seen in the sea lochs of the west of Scotland, in the Minch or in bays around the Hebrides. These flocks of divers make a splendid spectacle, especially when many of them have completed their spring moult. Perhaps the great northern diver is the most spectacular, and not only for its large size and striking plumage. The great northern divers that congregate in the north-west of Scotland and moult there in late winter are destined for breeding grounds in Iceland, Greenland and possibly Arctic Canada.

During the winter, many red-breasted mergansers occur well away from their breeding grounds in the north-west of the British Isles. These flocks decline as the numbers of mergansers on the bays and estuaries close to their breeding grounds increase during late winter. Then, in early spring, there is a final movement by those that nest inland to the breeding lakes and large rivers. Such movements can occasionally be noted from sea-watches (see page 94). For instance, on one day in late February, 86 were counted passing north off the Lleyn Peninsula of North Wales, and on another occasion two flocks totalling 132 were noted flying north through the Irish Sea between the Isle of Man and the Lancashire coast.

GREAT NORTHERN DIVER

GREAT CRESTED GREBE

♂

♀

RED-BREASTED
MERGANSER

For coastal birdwatchers one of the first signs of spring may be an increase in species like the grebes, divers and the red-breasted merganser, which begin to head to their breeding quarters in late February and early March.

Three winter ducks

One of the most interesting winter bird studies is to count on a regular basis – weekly if possible – the numbers of waterfowl on a local lake. Most of the species recorded will be commoner ones: but check these carefully, for scarcer waterfowl usually occur amongst the flocks of common ones.

Unless the lake shore and margins have been disturbed, there will usually be quite a marked zonal distribution of waterfowl. Most, including the coot, moorhen, mallard and teal, tend to concentrate in the weedbeds and very shallow water where they can dabble or up-end for their food. Only a few species that can dive deep will feed in deeper water.

The tufted duck and pochard are the commonest of diving ducks. Rarely do they come to land, other than when nesting, for their legs are positioned well back on their bodies, making them poor walkers. Both species breed in the British Isles, but neither is abundant. Recent estimates suggest breeding populations of about 6000–7000 pairs of tufted ducks and at least 200 and possibly as many as 400 pairs of pochards. During autumn, large numbers of tufted ducks and pochards visit the British Isles from breeding grounds in Scandinavia and the USSR. Thus, between September and January the numbers on a lake increase and then, from late winter though to April, the populations decline as the immigrants return to their foreign nesting grounds.

Tufted ducks and pochards appear to have similar behaviour, but the similarity is purely that of an ability to dive for food. Tufted ducks are almost entirely carnivorous, devouring invertebrates such as freshwater mussels and snails, bloodworms (the larvae of aquatic midges), and small crustaceans. Pochards are primarily herbivores, feeding mostly on the fruits and seeds of submerged waterweeds and, to a lesser extent, their shoots. Because the thickest weedbeds occur in shallow water, pochards feed in slightly shallower water than tufted ducks and rarely dive for food in water much deeper than 2 m, whereas tufted ducks will often dive 4–5 m.

It is interesting to time the dives of tufted ducks and pochards, especially when the water depth is known. The greater the depth, the longer the dive. This is probably simply because it takes the ducks that bit longer to reach their food on or close to the lake bed. Tufted ducks tend to remain submerged longer than pochards when diving in the same depth of water, possibly because they have to spend more time searching for their prey. (For instance, a tufted duck may dive for over 20 seconds at a depth of 2 m, compared to just 16 seconds for the pochard.) The plant foods of the pochard are not hidden in the mud or amongst the boulders of the lake bed as are the animal foods of the tufted duck.

Besides learning much about the commoner waterfowl, a regular study of a local lake will invariably provide the birdwatcher with the opportunity to see some much rarer species. For instance, a red-necked grebe may join the resident great crested grebes, or one day a black-throated diver might appear, driven inland from the sea by gales. One 'red-ribbon' duck, which occurs regularly on some reservoirs in south-eastern England but is quite scarce elsewhere, is the smew.

The smew is a 'sawbill': a fish-eating duck closely related to the commoner goosander and red-breasted merganser. Most of the smews recorded in the British Isles are red-headed females or immature, the beautiful black-and-white drakes being quite rare. They are usually seen close to the shore, often in shallow weedy bays, where their food – sticklebacks and smaller fish fry – tends to be concentrated.

TUFTED DUCK

POCHARD

SMEW

Count the numbers of waterfowl on your local lake as often as possible. Most will be commoner species, like the tufted duck and pochard; but something rarer – a smew, perhaps – may appear for a day or so.

Bird of the month: Chough

The chough is the rarest and perhaps most fascinating member of the crow family. It is easy to identify, from its glossy black plumage, round-fingered wings, sturdy orange-red legs and feet, and the fine, down-curved red bill, the latter specially adapted for probing in turf for small insects, particularly ants. But before it can be watched and identified, the chough must be located and this is easily done by listening for its characteristic call: a loud, very high-pitched 'keeaaar'.

This is chiefly a bird of rocky coasts and high sea cliffs, nesting in caves, cracks and crevices overlooking the sea. However, in North Wales several pairs nest in old slate quarries inland, and in the Isle of Man, Islay and western Ireland some pairs nest in ruined buildings away from the cliffs and in old lighthouses on the cliff top. Choughs rarely wander far from their nesting area, even in the middle of winter. Throughout the year they can be watched feeding on near-vertical cliff faces, amongst tussocks of thrift on the cliff top or on short turf just inland of the coast. Sometimes they may join with jackdaws or rooks out of the breeding season: any flock of crows close to chough habitat is worth checking through. In my first autumn visit to Islay I spent two days walking the cliffs in search of choughs but with no success. Then I happened to glance through a flock of crows feeding on the field next to the cottage I had rented in the middle of the island; amongst them were 11 choughs!

To watch wild choughs one must travel to the west coast. Good numbers still nest on Jura and Islay in the Hebrides. They are widespread in the Isle of Man, in North Wales west of the Conway Valley, and along the rocky coastline of West Wales. Many years ago, the chough nested along the entire coastline of Ireland, but has now withdrawn to the north, west and south coasts where it is still very common.

Why has the chough declined? There is no certain answer. Some have argued that competition with jackdaws is the reason; but jackdaws have different foods and different nest sites from the chough so there should not be any competition. Others have suggested that a series of very hard winters in the 19th century was the chief culprit, but if that were the case, why did not the hard winters of earlier centuries decimate the chough population then? Perhaps man has had an influence, through disturbance, egg collecting, shooting and reducing the feeding grounds in many areas by turning over the cliff-top pastures to arable crops.

Breeding begins in March when pairs that have bred before return to their old nest sites and those that are breeding for the first time pair and choose a nest site. Then the choughs are conspicuous as they display and collect nesting material. The eggs are usually laid in late April and from then, while the eggs are being incubated and the young raised, until mid-June when the young leave the nest, the choughs are much less conspicuous. Many people visit the Welsh island of Skomer, one of the most accessible chough sites in southern Britain, in this period to see the chough but most are disappointed or rewarded by a pair just flying overhead. Later, from July, they are easy to watch as family parties scour the cliffs for food and then join in loose flocks for the winter. But the best time of the year is March and early April, for then the cliffs are swarming with sea birds. The noise of the waves breaking at the cliff foot, and the clamour of the gulls, auks, cormorants, shags, kittiwakes and fulmars may be almost deafening, but the 'keeaaars' of the chough penetrate the din as a pair wheels above the cliff top. Magic!

The chough is one of our most fascinating resident birds, although it takes some finding, because of its very restricted distribution. It occurs in a most spectacular habitat. The bird's wild call, glossy black plumage and bright red bill and legs give it an exotic appearance.

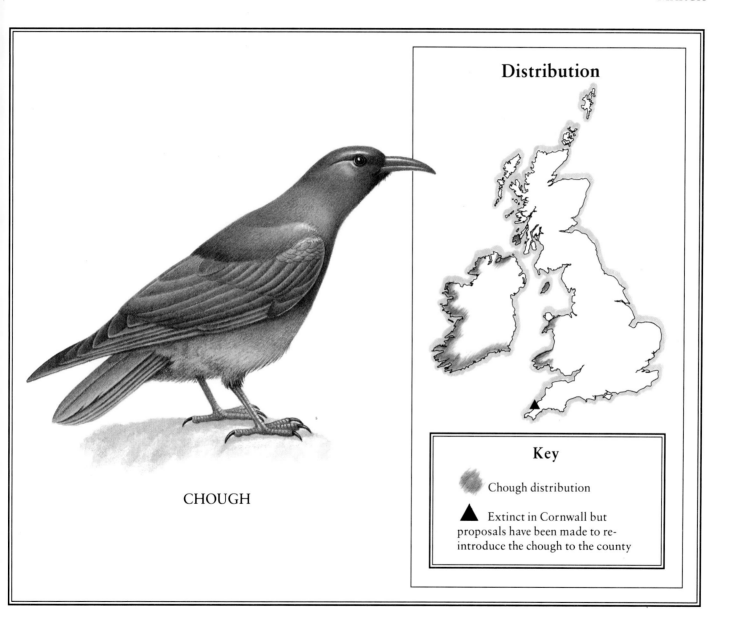

CHOUGH

Distribution

Key

Chough distribution

▲ Extinct in Cornwall but proposals have been made to re-introduce the chough to the county

Gaining a territory

Most species of birds are territorial in that before pairing and breeding occur, the male bird must acquire a plot of suitable land: his territory. If a male cannot obtain a territory, he must move on and try to obtain one elsewhere, for the birds that have a territory will not tolerate the presence of an unmated male in theirs. The altruistic human might suggest that all territories be made a little smaller so that every male could have one, but this would be suicidal for the future of the species. The size of the territory is that which can just support two adults and their young; if the territory was any smaller, then breeding success in the entire species would be lower. In some species, the size of the territory varies according to the quality of the habitat: pairs that live in areas that produce lots of food have smaller territories than those breeding in less productive areas.

However, sometimes an area could support more pairs of a particular species because there is lots of food available, but something else is lacking. This is illustrated well by certain woodland birds that nest in holes in trees. Let me explain this with a real instance of a wood in the Ribble Valley of Lancashire. In 1975, this wood had four great tit, one marsh tit, nine blue tit and one redstart territories. In 1976, 30 wooden nest boxes were put up in this wood and that year there were eight great tits, three marsh tits, 17 blue tits, five pied flycatcher and three redstart territories. What had prevented so many pairs from having territories in this wood before was the sparsity of nest holes in the trees. But then, when there was a superabundance of nest holes, males that formerly could not gain a territory did so, attracted a mate and bred. However, increasing the number of nest boxes further did not result in even more birds breeding in this wood, for by then the wood had been divided into the maximum number of territories and would support no more nesting pairs.

By mapping territories one can learn a great deal about our common breeding birds. It is simply a matter of noting on a map where the male birds are singing: this will give the numbers of pairs and the approximate centre of the territory. Then, through the spring and early summer, one looks for boundary clashes between neighbours, which are easier to observe in some species than others. Coots and mute swans are very aggressive and will swim to their territory boundaries as soon as their neighbour approaches his side of the invisible fence.

Dippers nest by and feed in streams, so they have a linear territory which is very easy to map. For example, choose a stream in the Pennines, and walk the entire river in a downstream direction. The dippers will fly downstream before you as you walk. But when they reach the end of their territory, they will turn back rather than risk a boundary skirmish with their neighbours. You now have the downstream territorial boundary of several pairs of dippers. Now repeat the exercise by walking upstream to discover the upper limits of the same territories.

Blackbird territories are also interesting to map, particularly in an area of suburban houses, playing fields and allotments. You will find that the area with houses will have the smallest blackbird territories, for their gardens and lawns are rich in food and this natural supply is supplemented by householders putting out extra food. Those territories that include some allotments will also be fairly small, for these well-cultivated plots support large populations of earthworms. But it is the open playing fields that will have the largest territories, because food is scarcer there and the territories must be large to provide enough for a family of blackbirds.

Right A pair of dippers on a moorland beck; the territories of such birds are easy to map. It is well worth studying the birds living in your 'patch' during spring, when they are actively seeking or defending territories.

Spring arrivals: some problems

Many birdwatchers enjoy searching for the first of the summer visitors, and particularly relish discovering a very early record that will make headlines in the local bird report. There are, however, several problems.

The nightjar was once much commoner than it is today. Certainly, every countryman knew the night-jar well enough to give it the alternative name of 'goatsucker', because it was thought to suck the milk from the farm goats. Unfortunately, the destruction of its scrubland habitat during the past 100 years has made the nightjar quite a scarce species today. So *finding* a nightjar is often quite a feat, and discovering the early bird is far more difficult than was formerly the case. The problem is exacerbated by the fact that the nightjar is a nocturnal species, in addition to which the characteristic 'churring' call of the male is often made only on the breeding territory. So unless the bird is flushed from its dense daytime cover, it will never be discovered. Nightjars are usually back on their breeding grounds in late April but any record for the beginning of the month is newsworthy.

The problem of seeing the bird should one be there also exists with the garganey, for this tiny duck tends to inhabit reed-fringed pools and spends most of the day hidden from view. So it may be that, even on a bird sanctuary that is carefully watched every day, a garganey may have been there for several days before it swims into open water and is noted. Garganeys usually return to Britain during the end of March and early April. However, there are several records for both January and February.

Since swifts are quite conspicuous and well-known birds, one would imagine that there are no problems in recording the earliest spring arrivals in the British Isles. The records would seem to bear this out, as most of them are from the extreme south of England where the birds make their first landfall after crossing the English Channel. So, the earliest is of a bird at Walton-on-the-Naze in Essex on 3 February, and the next at Telscombe in Sussex on 14 February. There are several early records during March and early April, before the normal time of arrival from the middle of April.

However, might not that Walton-on-the-Naze bird have been overlooked on 2 February, and the Telscombe bird on 13 February? And what about the birds recorded at Manchester on 28 March and a Midlothian swift recorded on 4 April? Were these the dates that the swifts concerned actually arrived in Britain? Surely they had arrived in southern England a day or two earlier, and been overlooked during their journey northwards?

The biggest problem is the cuckoo, for every retired colonel listens out carefully for the first so that he can dash a letter off to *The Times*! One aspect of the problem is that small boys are quite adept at deliberately imitating the cuckoo, while their normal, infuriating, high-pitched din, made on their way home after being released from school adds to the confusion by sounding from a distance like a cuckoo calling on a mild early spring afternoon! Accordingly, Robert Hudson, in the British Trust for Ornithology Guide, *Early and Late Dates for Summer Migrants*, commented: 'Only records of birds actually *seen* have been admitted, in order to remove all possible doubts about validity; the cuckoo's typical call-note is so easily imitated, e.g. by practical jokers, that this precaution seems advisable.'

The other aspect of the problem is that most people have no idea what a cuckoo looks like!

Hear and see a cuckoo before mid-March and you have a record to be proud of; just hear it and I'm afraid you have no record at all!

At the end of March, through April and into May keep your eyes and ears open for newly-arrived summer visitors. Keep a record of the dates on which they appear in your area.

SWIFT

NIGHTJAR

CUCKOO

GARGANEY

♀

♂

Birds of the upland streams

The upland rivers and streams of northern England, Scotland and Ireland have a quite special breeding bird community. Goosanders nest in holes in river-side trees or cliff faces and take their young down to the water soon after hatching; oystercatchers and sometimes ringed plovers nest on the bare shingle banks. Common sandpipers nest in the thick riverside grasses and herbs. Sand martin colonies have their nests in burrows in the eroding cliff-like banks, while grey wagtails and dippers build their nests in cracks and crannies amongst tree roots, riverside rock faces or bridge masonry. And kingfishers excavate their nesting holes in the bare clay of the river bank, usually close to suitable perches.

The density of these species (measured as the number of pairs per mile or kilometre) nesting along the streams is by no means constant, for the streams themselves are not constant. For instance, streams flowing over limestone produce far more food than those flowing over gritstone, and rivers with large areas of gravel-bottomed shallows allow for better feeding than deeper boulder-strewn rivers (see also page 48). Typical average densities, from rivers in northern England and Scotland, are as in the following table:

Mean number of pairs per 10 km

RIVER	Common Sandpiper	Kingfisher	Dipper	Grey Wagtail
Ribble	10.5	4.5	3.0	3.5
Hodder	11.0	5.0	5.0	6.0
Aire	9.7	3.3	3.3	6.6
Eden	12.5	5.0	10.0	7.5
Nith	4.0	2.0	4.0	6.0
Spey	6.0	0.0	2.0	2.0

However, large areas of a particular river may be devoid of pairs while other lengths have many more pairs than the average density suggests. For example, on the River Lune in Lancashire/Cumbria, one length of 4 km supported seven pairs of common sand-pipers, three pairs of kingfishers, five pairs of dippers and six pairs of grey wagtails, whereas another similar length of the same river had only two pairs of sandpipers and single pairs of dippers and grey wagtails.

Kingfishers are very dependent on the populations of small fish in the river. Although the trout and salmon angler might look with despair at a kingfisher plunging into one of their favourite pools and emerging with a tiny fish, they have no cause to worry, for the kingfisher eats mostly minnows. Where there are high minnow populations, there are thriving kingfisher populations.

Dippers feed almost exclusively on the inverte-brates of the river bed. These they catch by walking or diving into the shallows, grasping the bottom with their feet and using their wings to hold themselves against the current. Sometimes they will swallow smaller prey, such as mayfly and stonefly nymphs, as they gather them underwater. Bigger items, such as large caddis larvae, are taken to boulders where the dipper hammers them on the rock to kill and soften them. Lengths of river with large invertebrate popu-lations, and extensive gravel shallows where dippers can forage, always have the highest dipper populations.

In recent years there has been concern that the growing numbers of feral mink in our river valleys are reducing the populations of waterside birds.

GREY WAGTAIL

♀

♂

KINGFISHER

DIPPER

Upland streams are well worth a visit in spring, for there you will find species like the grey wagtail, dipper, kingfisher, common sandpiper, and perhaps the goosander.

Scrubland in spring

Scrubland is an intermediate stage between grassland and woodland. It includes habitats as diverse as gorse scrub on a moorland edge or sandy lowland heath, the heavily-overgrown wasteland of derelict industry and railway embankments, and the coastal scrub found on windswept cliff tops and mature sand dunes. The term 'scrub' might also include hedgerows and young tree plantations. Scrub is important, for it attracts species of birds that occur in high densities in no other habitat. The four species considered here are typical.

Stonechats are resident in the British Isles; the similar and closely-related whinchat (so called because it is commonly found in 'whin' or gorse scrub) is a summer visitor from Africa (see page 64). In the British Isles, the stonechat is primarily a bird of the west and south where the climate is mild. They commonly occur, for instance, amongst gorse on the cliffs of the Devon coast, on the dunes of West Wales and north-west England, and on the overgrown peat bogs of western Ireland. In severe winters the stonechat suffers, unlike the whinchat which is then enjoying a tropical climate. In the two very hard winters of 1961–62 and 1962–63 many inland populations were exterminated, and even in the milder areas they were decimated. J. T. R. Sharrock has described how, on Cape Clear Island off Co. Cork, Ireland, the 1961 population of up to 150 pairs fell to only three pairs in 1963 and 1964. In Lancashire, the inland stonechat population was reduced to just one male and the coastal dune population to three pairs in 1963. Subsequently, the populations have recovered, but with further set-backs following periods of harsh weather (as in 1979 and 1987).

Long-tailed tits, which breed also in open woodland as well as scrub, similarly suffer during harsh winters. In the winters of 1961–62 and 1962–63 the number of pairs nesting in one area of northern England fell from 87 to 23, a loss of almost 75 per cent. But long-tailed tits are quite prolific breeders, despite the fact that a large proportion of their fragile bottle-shaped nests are destroyed by predators. By 1966, this population had more than recovered to reach 91 pairs.

Whitethroats, like whinchats, are not affected by the British winters, for they overwinter in Africa. However, during the 1970s the populations of whitethroats in Britain crashed because of climatic conditions in central Africa. A series of drought years in the Sahel Zone resulted in a spread of desert conditions in the whitethroat's winter quarters and a large proportion perished. By the late 1970s, the whitethroat had become quite scarce in areas where it had been formerly common. Fortunately, an improvement of conditions in its African winter home allowed the whitethroat population to increase during the 1980s, but it is still not as common as it was in the 1960s.

Yellowhammers are amongst the best-known of British birds because of their song, 'a-little-bit-of-bread-and-no-cheese', (some males miss out the 'cheese'!). They are also widely distributed, occurring throughout the British Isles, except for the northern isles, the highest mountains, and the centres of the largest cities. They are also highly adaptable: there are instances of factory sites being abandoned by man and yellowhammers moving into the colonizing scrub within three years.

Despite occasional set-backs because of extreme weather, these four species, like those of many other scrubland birds such as the partridge, lesser whitethroat, whinchat, wheatear, meadow pipit and linnet, are still widespread and fairly common.

Areas of scrub, so often dismissed as 'wasteland', provide the nesting habitat for several species of bird. Is it not sad, therefore, that many landowners take great pains to clear all these 'untidy' corners?

STONECHAT

LONG-TAILED TIT

WHITETHROAT

YELLOWHAMMER

Bird of the month: Capercaillie

Like the white-tailed sea eagle, the present Scottish population of capercaillie is the result of a reintroduction following the species' extinction. It had disappeared from England certainly by the end of the 14th century, though records are very sparse. Through to the end of the 17th century it remained a common species in the extensive pine forests of Scotland and Ireland, but deforestation brought it to the verge of extinction in the mid-1700s, and the last few were killed by hunters. In Scotland, a few survived in Speyside to at least 1771 and in Deeside to 1785, whilst the Irish population was finally exterminated about 1790. During the 19th century, several attempts at reintroductions in Scotland were unsuccessful, but in 1837 and 1838 a total of 13 cocks and 29 hens were brought from Sweden to Taymouth Castle, Perthshire, by Lord Breadalbane; these bred successfully and quickly colonized the surrounding forests. Further introductions by Victorian landowners in Fife, Angus, Aberdeenshire and Inverness-shire resulted, by 1914, in a thriving population from central Scotland north and east to the Moray Firth.

The capercaillie is the largest of the grouse family and depends largely on pines for its survival. In winter and early spring it feeds almost exclusively on pine shoots, needles, cones and seeds. The rest of the year its taste is rather more catholic, and includes also forest fruits, grasses, heather, and the fruits, shoots and leaves from a wide variety of trees. Where there is arable land close to the forest, they will also eat cereals, turnips and brassica leaves. Sadly, because of the damage they do, many foresters and farmers in the Scottish valleys consider capercaillie a pest.

Despite their relatively huge size, capercaillie are not the easiest of species to locate. For most of the year they are quite shy, retiring birds which depart rapidly when humans approach. Even the most careful stalk is often rewarded just by the sight of a capercaillie taking two or three running strides before it takes flight and crashes away through the tree tops.

However, in spring, from early April, the cock capercaillie begin to display and then they are invariably bold and sometimes violently aggressive to anything other than a hen capercaillie that strays close to their display stand in the forest clearings.

This aggression is graphically described by Kenneth Richmond, who found a cock caper displaying on a knoll at the edge of a pine forest in Glen Lyon and approached to within ten yards to take a photograph: 'It came trundling towards me, trailing its wings on the ground, fairly shivering with rage. Thrusting its horny, white beak in my face (I was crouching to get a photograph) it erupted in a glottal belch: *kik-ek kik-kik-ek er up GURRUP* – tossing its head with a flourish at the last syllable. This was too much of a good thing, I thought, retreating hastily. But not hastily enough. Following me with a rush, the bird grabbed me by the trousers bottoms and began belabouring me with his bony wings – great, cracking blows which left my shins and calves black and blue for weeks. Not satisfied with this, it seized me by the hand and although I was wearing thick leather gloves at the time tore a gaping hole in the fleshy part of my right thumb.... Breaking into a trot, I ran as fast as my legs would carry me, only to find the insensate bird pursuing me. Taking off when it saw me gaining ground, it flew straight at me, thumping me in the small of the back and knocking me face-down in the heather. There it renewed its flogging.' (David Banneman, *Birds of the British Isles.*)

This bird later took to waylaying the local bus, but came to grief when it attacked a Land Rover travelling at 65 mph!

The story of the capercaillie, the most ferocious bird of the forests of northern Scotland, is one of extinction and then of successful reintroduction.

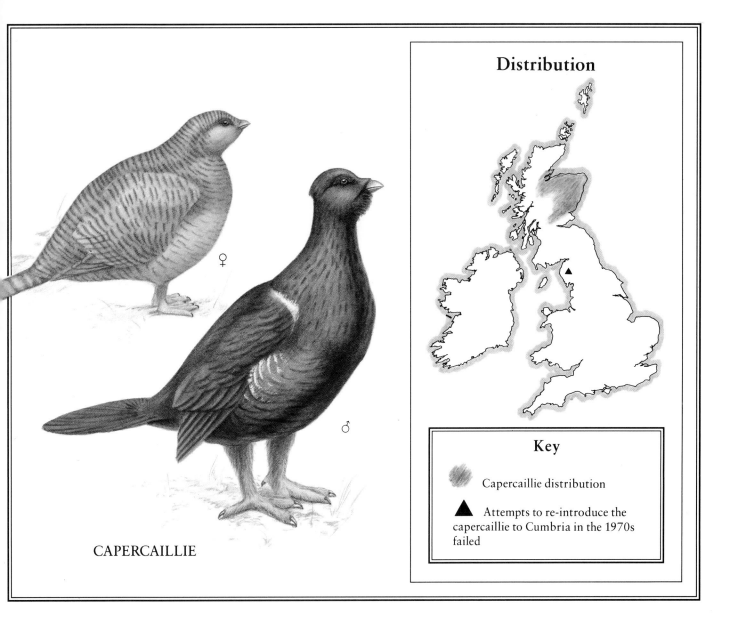

Distribution

CAPERCAILLIE

Key

Capercaillie distribution

▲ Attempts to re-introduce the capercaillie to Cumbria in the 1970s failed

Spring migration

Whilst the spring migration is less noted than the autumn migration for massive 'falls' of migrants at coastal bird observatories, or for the occurrence of large numbers of rare or scarce species, it is in some ways more interesting than the autumn passage. In spring, most migrants are adults in summer plumage, whereas most autumn migrants are juveniles, born the previous spring and summer; and adults in summer plumage are much easier to identify, and often more attractive to watch, than immatures. In addition, the males are often conspicuously in full song at this time, whether they are going to nest in the British Isles or move further north to breed, whereas in autumn many birds are difficult to locate as they skulk silently in undergrowth.

Thus, a visit to Dungeness (Kent), Portland Bill (Dorset), Bardsey Island (Gwynedd), Spurn Head (Humberside) or Fair Isle (Shetland) in spring may reveal rare species, like the woodchat shrike, golden oriole, subalpine warbler, rustic bunting and scarlet rosefinch, in their bright summer plumage and the males perhaps in song. And commoner birds, like the blackcap and pied flycatcher, will be in full breeding plumage, unlike the drab youngsters one might watch in autumn.

No matter where you live, the arrival of spring migrants is generally more noticeable than the departure of autumn migrants. A daily walk around an area of woodland, scrub, coastal headland or reed fen will reveal the migrants when they arrive. One day there are no chiffchaffs or willow warblers singing in the trees, or whitethroats and whinchats in the gorse and brambles. But the next day they seem to be everywhere: they arrived silently, during the night. 'One swallow does not make a summer', so it is said, yet the first sight of one flying past is something to highlight in the diary. And everybody listens carefully through April in the hope that they will be the first to hear the male cuckoo.

We can all make a list of the first date of arrival. Indeed, it is interesting to do this for our common summer visitors, and over the years compare these dates. Yet how many of us can produce a similar list of 'last dates' in autumn for the swallow, house and sand martin, swift, willow warbler, chiffchaff, wheatear, blackcap and so on?

If one keeps a bird diary for several years, it is interesting to note how the date of arrival for a particular species is remarkably consistent for a specific part of the country, and how different species arrive on different dates. The first arrivals are usually chiffchaffs, wheatears and sand martins. In North Devon I used to find the first of these on about 23 March, but in Lancashire I have to wait until about the 28th. Similarly, in Devon I always used to see my first swallow by the end of March, whereas in Lancashire they usually arrive in the first week of April. Such geographical variations must always be borne in mind when you are compiling a personal list of dates of arrival: the further south an observer is, the earlier will be these dates.

At the same time, it is important to keep up regular observations. It is no good going to the shore on 28 April and noting sandwich, common and arctic terns for the first time in the year and recording these as 'dates of arrival' if that was your first April visit. The sandwich terns may have been there since the 1st, the common terns since the 16th and arctic terns since the 25th. So choose an area close to home – somewhere with woodland and an area of open water – and have a daily walk, preferably in the early morning when the males will be in full song. Then you will have the precise dates of arrival.

Right The cuckoo, which arrives from Africa about the middle of April. Nothing typifies spring for the birdwatcher as much as the first cuckoo, or a party of swallows reaching the south coast from the English Channel, or a group of terns passing northwards along the edge of the tide.

Sea-bird colonies

A visit to a big sea-bird nesting colony is a highlight in any birdwatcher's year. However, to visit some of the most spectacular colonies needs thorough planning.

Gannets are very easy to watch from the mainland as they fly offshore, but a visit to a gannetry can be difficult to arrange since most are on remote islands, such as Sula Sgeir and St Kilda off north-west Scotland, Bass Rock in the Forth, Grassholm off the Pembrokeshire peninsula, and so on. Some are a little more accessible, such as the relatively new gannetry on Fair Isle in the Shetlands, or the one on Bempton Cliffs on the Humberside coast.

A day spent watching the antics of the nesting gannets is quite exciting even though the fishy stench can be quite appalling. Gannets are territorial in that they build their nests of seaweed just far enough apart so that birds sitting on adjacent nests cannot quite reach one another with their powerful, dagger-like bills. This, one would imagine, should ensure peaceful co-existence. Not at all! When an adult gannet wishes to go to sea, it ritually raises its bill skywards to let its neighbours know its intentions, and takes off. But on its return, it must land directly on its nest or else be attacked. Such a direct landing is difficult to achieve, and returning gannets often land a few yards away from their nest, suffering fierce attacks in consequence. Later in the season, any young gannets that stray even a few inches from their nest will receive a severe thrashing from their neighbours.

Manx shearwaters are much more difficult to observe. There are many famous shearwater colonies, such as Skokholm and Skomer off the Pembrokeshire coast and Bardsey off the Lleyn Peninsula of North Wales, but in a daytime visit little, if anything, will be seen of the thousands of shear-waters. These birds nest deep underground in burrows, and because gulls are keen to catch and eat shearwaters, they will only come to land, to change places when incubating their single egg or to feed their chick, when it is fully dark. So, to watch them, an overnight stay is necessary. But it is well worth it! As the sun goes down, large rafts of shearwaters, which have been away feeding on sardines as far afield as the Bay of Biscay, gather offshore. Then, when it is dark, they come ashore uttering the most blood-curdling range of hoarse nasal screams and hoots. The air above the island is a mass of blurred black-and-white missiles that will collide with you if you get in their way! Throughout the night, birds come and go, with rushes of wings and piercing cries, but by dawn no sign remains of the nocturnal activity, save for the now-silent burrows.

Puffins are perhaps the most popular of sea birds, with their clown-like bills and morning-suit plumage. There are several small puffinries on the rocky parts of the British mainland. However, the larger and more spectacular colonies are on offshore islands such as Skomer, the Farnes, the Isle of May, and in Orkney and Shetland. Like the shearwaters, puffins nest in burrows, but like the gannets they are active during the day.

Puffins are most interesting to watch when they are courting or when they are feeding their young. Then they return to land with several small sand-eels carefully arranged sideways in their large bills. Gulls parade the cliff top, eager to intercept these birds and obtain an easy meal. The puffins know this. They will fly in circles over the burrows and then land and rush quickly underground. Occasionally, the gull wins and the puffin must go to sea to gather more fish. More often, the puffin wins and you are left with the amusing sight of a gull peering into the puffin's burrow as if to say: 'I know you're in there!'

PUFFIN

MANX
SHEARWATER

GANNET

All birdwatchers
look forward to
visiting a big
sea-bird colony
and watching at
close quarters
birds that usually
stay well out at
sea. Some species,
like the puffin, are
fairly easy to see.
Others, like the
gannet and Manx
shearwater, call
for a little more
effort because of
the remoteness of
their colonies.

Spring warblers

One of the most pleasant birdwatching tasks of spring is recording all the warbler species that visit the British Isles for the summer. Spring is the ideal time to do this because the birds are never more easy to watch closely. In spring they are in their brightest plumage, plus they occur in fixed territories in what the textbooks describe as their usual habitats, and the males sing loudly and often conspicuously. By contrast, after the end of June warblers tend to be far more inconspicuous and silent.

At least one visit must be made to an extensive area of reedbeds. There, in the middle of the reeds, will be reed warblers and, usually, where reeds give way to canary-grass, sedges and rushes, the sedge warbler. Both of these are quite easy to find and identify. However, the third member of the trio, the grasshopper warbler, is a bit more tricky. A long, drawn-out, high-pitched trill, which may last continuously for a minute or more, from rank grass or tussock sedge at the edge of the reed fen, betrays its presence. Seeing a grasshopper warbler can be very difficult, for they are so secretive. At first light on a late May morning, however, the males often climb to the top of a tussock to utter their characteristic 'song'.

Woodland warblers are sometimes much more difficult because the males often insist on singing from the tops of the tree canopy. There they are camouflaged amongst the leaves and, even worse, the observer has to look up to them against the light, so silhouettes are the commonest views. Unless the different songs of the male warblers are familiar to the observer, the identification of the birds can be most frustrating. Beyond any doubt, the best line of attack is to find one male warbler singing and listen carefully to it while time is spent seeking to identify the songster. Then both song and bird are learnt together. But this takes patience!

There are, however, certain clues that help. Take the three leaf warblers first. On their breeding grounds they have subtly different habitats. The willow warbler rarely occurs in the middle of a wood or amongst dense trees – it is far more a bird of the open glade or woodland edge. Often it occurs away from real woodland, in scrub and amongst lines of coppiced willows or alders close to a river or lake. Its song, too, is quite conspicuous and easy to learn: a descending liquid trill.

By contrast, the chiffchaff and wood warbler are birds of the forest and thick woodland. Chiffchaffs occur in a wider range of wood than wood warblers, the latter being especially partial to very old oak and beech trees. Where the undergrowth is lush, there chiffchaffs will predominate, while wood warblers are often very numerous in areas of woodland that are almost devoid of ground vegetation. Chiffchaffs are easy to identify by their 'chiff-chiff-chaff' song, but the wood warbler's song is so characteristic that once heard it will never be forgotten: a 'shivering trill' that begins with the slow repetition of one note but becomes faster, 'stip . . . stip . . . stip . . . stip . . . stititititititiptiptweeeeeeee'.

Both garden warblers and blackcaps are birds of open woodlands, usually where there are large patches of brambles, wild roses and other low shrubs. These two warblers, which often occur in close proximity, frequently have such similar songs that only a trained ear can separate them. And although these songs are often made from dense cover, making the songster difficult to see, in the early morning males of both species frequently proclaim their territorial rights from fairly open positions. Then, identification is easy, for the plumage of the birds is more different than chalk is from cheese.

Of all bird groups perhaps none provides greater problems of identification than the warblers. The secret, as far as the commoner species are concerned, is to seek them at dawn in spring when they are tied to a territory and make themselves conspicuous by singing loudly.

GARDEN
WARBLER

CHIFFCHAFF

WOOD WARBLER

BLACKCAP

The moorland edge

Too many people who visit an area of moorland for a birdwatching holiday leave the valley and rush as quickly as their legs will carry them to the summit plateaux in the belief that this is where the more interesting hill birds are to be found. It is true that the extensive sweeping expanses of heather, cotton-grass and peat bog provide the nesting habitat for species like the red grouse, golden plover and dunlin, but by ignoring the slope below the summits many important species will be overlooked.

What makes the lower moorland slopes so attractive to several species of birds is the variety of feeding and nesting niches to be found there. Many streams well up on the slopes in small peaty pools before making their way downhill to the valley. In some areas, the streams have cut their way into the hillside to create steep ravines (known as 'cloughs' in Lancashire and north-west Yorkshire) or sheer-faced limestone gorges. Because of their relative inaccessibility to that scourge of moorland vegetation, the sheep, and the shelter they afford from the drying winds, these allow tall and lush vegetation to grow at great altitudes: alders, bird cherry and sycamore, and a wide variety of lowland herbs. On the slopes, soil 'creeps' downhill, so that lower down several metres may have accumulated. This allows for the growth of scattered shrubs, brambles and dense stands of bracken. Higher up, there is often a scattering of boulders that have been broken from the bedrock through centuries of frost and ice action.

This mosaic attracts some of the most special of moorland birds. It is, for example, the main upland natural nesting ground of three species of the thrush family that are summer visitors to the British Isles: the ring ouzel, wheatear and whinchat.

Ring ouzels are entirely restricted to the uplands of northern and western Britain. Their single or double fluting song frequently echoes across the lower slopes in April and May. However, they are quite shy birds and will quickly depart at long range with a 'chak–chak' call when alarmed. Usually they nest close by the rocky ravines of the juvenile streams, on a rock ledge or amongst a heather tussock.

Wheatears and whinchats are far more bold and conspicuous. Wheatears require holes for nesting, and so the boulder-strewn slopes provide ideal territories. By contrast, whinchats seek areas of thicker vegetation, areas of bracken, bramble, and stunted hawthorns and gorse on the lower slopes. Following a series of mild winters that have allowed the resident stonechat populations to increase (see page 54), stonechats too may colonize the same habitat as the whinchat. When this happens, the stonechats tend to occur in areas of gorse, leaving the other lower-slope niches for the whinchats.

The late Lawrence Eccles spent many years studying the bird populations of the slopes of Lancashire's Bowland Fells. In one area, covering about a quarter of a square mile, he discovered three pairs of ring ouzels, seven pairs of wheatears and 16 pairs of whinchats. Most fell walkers, intent on reaching the higher ground, might never encounter a single one!

The lower fell slopes are also the nesting grounds for many other species. In northern England and parts of Scotland the twite is often referred to as the mountain linnet; however, they tend not to nest on the summits of moor and mountain, but on the lower slopes. Many birds of prey, though they may hunt the open moor, prefer to nest on the lower slopes where there is often a much higher density and variety of prey: species like the short-eared owl, merlin and hen harrier. And those that do nest on the higher ground often move on to the lower slopes to hunt.

WHEATEAR

♂

♀

WHINCHAT

♂

♀

RING OUZEL

♂

♀

The high moorlands of northern and western Britain are worth visiting because of their unique bird community. But do not neglect the lower slopes, especially if you want to see the ring ouzel, whinchat and wheatear.

Bird of the month: Bluethroat

May sees the last arrivals of those birds that have wintered in the tropics and will spend the spring and summer nesting and raising their young in the British Isles. It is also perhaps the main month when other species also head northwards to breed, not in Britain, but elsewhere in Europe and the Arctic. For some of these, Britain may be on their migration route and they may stop off here for a short while, replenishing their food reserves, before embarking on the last leg of their long journey. For example, several thousands of sanderlings, which winter as far away as southern Africa and breed off the Arctic tundra of Canada, Greenland and Siberia, halt their journey for a few weeks in May on the Irish Sea coast of northern England. These are predictable annual events – stopovers by true passage migrants.

However, there are several other species that also head northwards but whose usual route takes them well to the east of the British Isles, or whose migration ends to the south of them. These would not normally be expected here. In most years, though, some do arrive, usually as a result of meteorological conditions. By waiting for the right weather conditions, and going at once to one of the famous coastal bird observatories or reserves, there is every chance that one or more of these scarcer passage migrants will have arrived.

There are two different forms or subspecies of bluethroat. In one, the male's blue 'throat' or breast has a white spot in the middle. These white-spotted bluethroats nest to the south and east of the British Isles, from central Spain, north to Belgium and Denmark, and east to the Baltic and western USSR.

For them to arrive on the British coast they must overshoot their breeding areas on spring migration: they must go too far to the north-west. Typical 'overshoot' conditions would include a stiff southerly wind that will carry the birds further north, and overcast skies at night to make navigation difficult. Other birds that may similarly overshoot their destination and arrive in Britain in spring include the tawny pipit, golden oriole, hoopoe, spoonbill, purple heron, great reed warbler, roller, alpine swift and bee-eater.

By contrast, the other form, the red-spotted bluethroat, has, as its name implies, a red spot in the middle of the blue breast in the male. This form breeds further north, from Scandinavia and across northern Russia and Siberia.

May is the ideal month to spend a holiday at one of the bird observatories, for not only is there a good chance of one of these rarer species appearing, but there are sure to be plenty of commoner migrants passing through, and possibly even something much rarer. All of the observatories listed below have facilities for residential visitors.

Bird observatories:
1. Fair Isle (Shetland)
2. Isle of May (Fife)
3. Spurn Head (Humberside)
4. Sandwich Bay (Kent)
5. Dungeness (Kent)
6. Portland Bill (Dorset)
7. Lundy Island (Devon)
8. Cape Clear Island (Co. Cork, Ireland)
9. Bardsey Island (Gwynedd)
10. South Walney (Cumbria)

Other outstanding sites include Cley and Blakeney Point, Norfolk (11); Minsmere and Walberswick, Suffolk (12); Skomer and Skokholm Islands, off Pembrokeshire (13); Selsey Bill, West Sussex (14); and Flamborough Head, Humberside (15); Lindisfarne, off Northumberland (16).

All birdwatchers like to see the unusual. It is well worth visiting one of the bird observatories on the south and east coasts in May, for that is where species like the rare bluethroat may turn up.

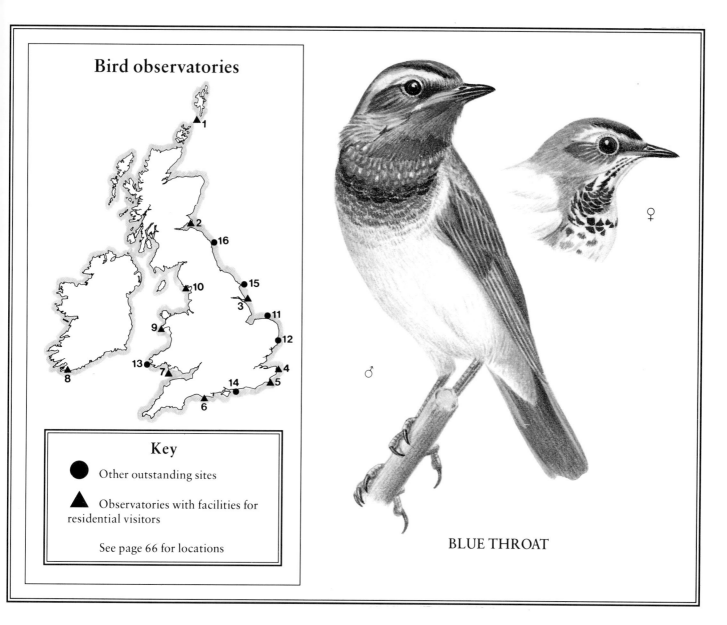

Bird observatories

Key

● Other outstanding sites

▲ Observatories with facilities for residential visitors

See page 66 for locations

BLUE THROAT

Rare breeding birds

There is nothing quite like watching rare birds. The easiest and most accessible of rare birds to watch are rare breeding birds, whose advantage lies in the fact that they can generally be guaranteed, because they are tied down to a nest site.

However, and I cannot stress this enough: disturbance can make rare birds extinct birds! Never should a birdwatcher disturb a rare bird on its breeding grounds. It is possible to watch most of Britain's rare breeding birds – from Cetti's warblers to greenshanks, from snow buntings to harriers and eagles – at a distance, without the birds being a alarmed. Should the birds be alarmed, then move away immediately.

Rare breeding birds fall into one of perhaps six categories, though there is some overlap between them. Some were once quite common and widespread throughout the British Isles but have declined naturally, possibly because of climatic changes. These would include species like the wryneck and red-backed shrike. A second category are those that are rare because their habitat is limited in the British Isles: this would include species like the dotterel and snow bunting that nest in arctic niches on the highest mountains. The third category includes species whose habitat has decreased, often as a result of habitat destruction by man. Fenland and marshland birds such as the marsh harrier and bittern are classic examples. So too are the ruff, avocet and black-tailed godwit which bred in Britain into the 19th and early 20th centuries, but then became extinct before re-colonizing in the 1940s, 1950s and 1960s.

Some species are rare because the British Isles is at the edge of their natural range. The black-necked grebe, which is quite common in eastern Europe, or the Slavonian grebe, which breeds from Iceland, through Scandinavia, the Baltic countries and the USSR, have outposts here of just a few pairs. The Kentish plover was in this category, when it bred on the English Channel coast until 1956, but it has since retreated to Europe and the Channel Islands.

By contrast, some species have recently extended their range to include Britain: species like the little gull, which first attempted to nest on the Ouse Washes in 1975; the Mediterranean gull, which first bred at Needs Oar Point in Hampshire in 1968; and the serin, which, following a spread northwards through Europe from 1800, finally colonized southern England in 1967. It appears that several Scandinavian species are also in the process of extending their range to northern Britain. The redwing first bred in Scotland in 1925 and the fieldfare in 1967: both species now appear to be well established and spreading. In recent years, the great northern diver, snowy owl, shore lark, bluethroat and lapland bunting have certainly nested, but it remains to be seen whether they consolidate their status here.

Unfortunately, some of the most spectacular of our rare breeding birds are rare simply and solely because of human persecution. The red kite was once widespread and common but persecution in the 19th century saw its extermination in England, Scotland and much of Wales. At the beginning of the 20th century only three pairs were left, in central Wales. Careful protection by the RSPB and Nature Conservancy, in the face of continued set-backs at the hands of egg-collectors and poisoning by farmers and gamekeepers, has slowly averted the kite's extinction and the future of this magnificent bird seems assured.

The same happy ending was not to be for the white-tailed eagle. This had been harried ruthlessly to extinction by the early years of the 20th century (the last nested on Shetland in 1910).

Right A peregrine chases a rare white-tailed sea eagle above their nesting cliffs in the Hebrides. Rare breeding birds are rigorously protected by law, and severe penalties await those found guilty of disturbing them. However it is possible to watch some of our rarest breeders without causing any disturbance.

Sea-bird cliffs

One of the most exciting places for any birdwatcher is a high, sheer cliff, thronged with sea birds. As one reaches the cliff edge and gazes across the cliff face, the first impressions are of sheer numbers and the incredible din caused by the cries of the birds and the sea thundering against the rocks below. But, then, as one settles down and looks carefully through the binoculars, a pattern slowly unfolds from the apparent chaos.

Each species of sea bird has its own niche on the cliff. On the wider ledges and hidden in the recesses of sea caves are the shags and cormorants, on their large nests composed of piles of rotting seaweed. The guillemots line up, in close ranks, on the narrower ledges. One wonders how the guillemots manage to incubate a large egg and then to raise their young in such a dangerous position. But the pear-shaped eggs are constructed so that if they are knocked accidentally, they do not roll off the ledge but spin, pirouette-fashion, on the one spot.

Higher on the cliff, on slightly wider ledges than are commonly used by the guillemots, one finds the fulmars – the albatrosses of the Atlantic, which soar (when they are not feeding at sea or sitting on their single egg) on stiff wings alongside the cliff face. Fulmars are very interesting birds. Up to 1878 they nested in the British Isles only on the remote St Kilda archipelago, and were quite rare visitors to most areas. Then a population explosion occurred. Quickly, fulmars have colonized most of the cliffs of Britain and Ireland and are now one of our commonest sea birds.

Kittiwakes also nest on the ledges, but they do not rely on them entirely to hold their eggs and young. Instead, they construct large nests from seaweed that is glued together and attached firmly on to the cliff with mud and their white droppings. Like most species of sea birds, kittiwakes are communal nesters. So, on a particular cliff, the nests will be concentrated in one area while the rest of the cliff, which might contain just as suitable ledges, is ignored.

Many cliff-nesting birds prefer to nest hidden away in a deep recess or burrow. Cracks of all shapes and sizes throughout the cliff from sea-level upwards provide the razorbills with their nest sites. Similar crevices on the cliffs of the Isle of Man and around the coasts of Ireland and northern and western Scotland are used by the black guillemot, or 'tystie'. Puffins may excavate their nesting burrows in the turf covering the cliff top.

Most gulls do not nest on sheer cliff faces, though sometimes there may be several pairs of herring gulls or a pair of great black-backed gulls on the broader ledges, especially in areas where the countryside inland of the cliff coast is disturbed. On the famous 'sea-bird islands', such as Skomer, Skokholm and the Isle of May, most gulls nest on the flat ground or slopes behind the cliffs.

Two words of warning are essential for those who are intending to visit a big sea-bird cliff. The first is to go at the right time of the year. Guillemots and razorbills take their young to the sea when they are only a few days old: they simply encourage the tiny birds to jump from their nests and then they swim with them far offshore. Shags will sometimes begin breeding in late winter and finish earlier than might be expected. So to see all the birds there, it is essential to make a visit no later than the end of June. In July and August all that may remain are the fulmars and the massive cliff face coated with guano.

The second point is that each year people die from slipping over the edge of cliffs. Be adequately shod and take care.

SHAG

KITTIWAKE

FULMAR

If you want to enjoy the sight of thousands of sea birds on their breeding cliffs, go no later than the end of June.

Hole-nesting woodland birds

Several species of woodland birds nest in holes in trees. Blue and great tits are perhaps the most widespread and best known. Coal tits also nest throughout the British Isles, though they tend to prefer coniferous woodlands as does the crested tit, which is restricted to the remains of the old Caledonian pine forests of northern Scotland. The very similar marsh and willow tits, which are best distinguished from each other by their calls, are restricted to England, Wales and southern Scotland. Listen for the diagnostic 'pitchuu' call off the marsh tit, and the nasal 'zi-zurr-zi-zurr' of the willow tit. Marsh tits occur mainly in mature broad-leaved woodland where they choose existing holes for their nests, whereas the willow tit frequents birch, alder and willow woodlands and excavates its nest hole in an old rotting tree trunk.

Small holes and cavities in tree trunks are also used by two summer visitors, the redstart and pied flycatcher. One problem that these two species face is that often all the nest holes in a wood are occupied when they return to the British Isles from Africa in late April. Many woodlands that have few redstarts and pied flycatchers, or none at all, could have several pairs if there were more nest holes available (see page 48). Bigger holes, both in tree trunks and amongst the roots at the base of trees, are often used by larger birds. Tawny and little owls and kestrels, for instance, often use such nest sites.

Two species that are increasing along tree-lined rivers and lakes in Britain are the goldeneye and goosander. Both nest in holes in trees. The goldeneye is still quite rare, nesting only in a few lakeside forests in the Scottish Highlands and in Cumbria's Lake District. But if the spread of the goosander is anything to go by, then this beautiful duck may soon be found nesting throughout much of the British Isles.

The major problem, though, is the shortage of holes in trees. In the modern coniferous forests, the trees are harvested long before they can 'deteriorate' and develop cracks and holes for nesting birds. In many of the larger broad-leaved woodlands, the forester is constantly looking out for oak, ash and beech trees that are reaching peak size and condition for the timber trade, and then replanting with saplings. So, few trees are permitted to pass maturity and develop fungal rot that would, in time, create cavities in the valuable wood of the tree trunk. The answer to this problem lies with the birdwatcher and nest boxes: artificial holes.

Many people who have a garden put a nest box in a tree for the local blue tits to nest in. But most could go further by putting up extra nest boxes in the hope of attracting a pair of great tits or tree sparrows to the garden. And should there be a particularly large tree, a bigger box, measuring about 2 ft × 1 ft × 1 ft with a big hole in the side, might attract a pair of tawny owls to the garden.

Perhaps even more satisfying may be to construct a lot of nest boxes of different dimensions, using relatively inexpensive recycled timber, in the early winter and obtain permission to put them up in a local private wood where they will not be damaged by vandals. The boxes should be put up in the trees no later than the beginning of December so that they are part of the woodland furniture well before our resident species are choosing nest sites. Certainly, the populations of tits will increase; perhaps redstarts and pied flycatchers will be attracted to nest there as well. If the wood is close to a river several large boxes may attract a pair of goosanders, and if the wood is by a lake then a female goldeneye may decide that it is the perfect place for her eggs.

REDSTART

PIED
FLYCATCHER

GREAT TIT

In November and December make as many nest boxes as you can and seek permission to put them up in January in an area of woodland to which the public has no access. Many will be occupied in spring by great and blue tits. You might also attract redstarts and pied flycatchers to your wood.

Summer on the heather moors

Well-managed heather moorland, where the heather is carefully burned off in strips in an annual rotation, is a quite special habitat with a unique community of breeding birds. The most important member of the community is possibly the red grouse, for it is this species that gives the heather moor its alternative name of 'grouse moor', and it is for the grouse that so much time and energy is spent maintaining the quality of the moor. Of course, the end product is grouse shooting. But it must be pointed out that without the carefully controlled shooting and management there would be little heather moor and few grouse in the British Isles. Either the moor would deteriorate, as so many have since the decline in the numbers of gamekeepers since 1914, or it would be made economically 'productive' in other ways such as forestry or intensive sheep grazing, which would also ruin the heather and decimate the grouse.

In early summer, the breeding cycle of the red grouse is nearing its end, as most clutches are laid in April or May, most have hatched by early June, and the young can fly strongly when only two weeks old. The grouse population is then at its peak and will decline after 12 August, 'the Glorious Twelfth', when shooting commences, and even more so later in the autumn when the cocks establish their territories and expel the excess birds.

However, most birdwatchers visit heather moors to watch other species. Birds of prey are probably most important. Although golden eagles, peregrines, buzzards and kestrels often feed over heather moorland, two species are more intimately linked with this habitat than any other: the merlin and hen harrier.

During the end of the 19th century and first half of the 20th century, hen harriers were persecuted to such an extent that they became restricted to the more remote hills of northern Scotland, the Hebrides and Orkney Isles and Ireland. Following the enforcement of the Bird Protection Act of 1954 and subsequent legislation, they have slowly increased and extended their range through much of Scotland, onto the Pennine moors of northern England, and into Wales. Unfortunately, persecution has not yet ceased. Each year several nests are vandalized by imbeciles who imagine that hen harriers nesting on their moors will damage the grouse stocks. These criminals need to be told that the harriers seek small prey, especially voles and small songbirds, and *not* the grouse.

Short-eared owls have also suffered from persecution, though not to the same extent as the hen harrier. This owl has probably survived because, although it commonly nests on heather moor and is still persecuted there, it also nests in other moorland habitats where there are no grouse and few gamekeepers. They frequently nest in young conifer plantations (as do, increasingly, hen harriers). Both species do a splendid job here for the foresters, by devouring large numbers of short-tailed voles. Short-eared owls also often nest on the lower slopes, in bracken stands and even in dense rushes in upland pastures. And although they are very conspicuous birds compared with other owls because they hunt through the day, they are extremely adept at keeping the location of their nests secret. For example, in the Tyne Valley one pair nested in a field next to a farmhouse without the farmer knowing it! Each day he passed within 20 yards of the incubating bird!

Certainly, the highlight of a summer visit to a heather moor is of sitting in the sun, with grouse calling 'go-back ... go-back' all around, hen harriers and short-eared owls quartering the hillside, and the blue flash of a merlin shooting past in pursuit of a meadow pipit.

HEN
HARRIER

♀

♂

SHORT-EARED
OWL

♂

♀

A summer visit to a heather moor will be dominated by the calls of red grouse. You may also be rewarded with the sight of hunting hen harriers and short-eared owls. Watch, but do not disturb them.

RED GROUSE

Bird of the month: Little ringed plover

In the drought of 1938, the level of a reservoir at Tring, Hertfordshire, fell as water was pumped out to maintain the level of the Grand Union Canal. On 5 June, a pair of little ringed plovers were identified, and these were carefully watched through to 14 August as they nested and raised three young. This was 'a bolt from the blue'; an unprecedented event, for prior to this the species had only been a rare vagrant to the British Isles. Though six individual little ringed plovers were recorded in the following five years, it was not until 1944 that the next breeding took place. Again, this was on the Tring Reservoirs when the water level fell in the spring of that year and two pairs bred. A third also nested in 1944, on a gravel pit in Middlesex.

From the end of the Second World War, the British construction industry required huge amounts of gravel for national reconstruction and then modernization of the country. Concrete was needed for buildings, the renovation of old roads and the later construction of the motorway system. So from about 1945, many hundreds of lowland sites were excavated for gravel deposits, leaving behind flooded gravel pits. These were ideal nesting sites for little ringed plovers and the British population quickly increased and spread. E. R. Parrinder, who studied this increase, reported that by 1959 – just two decades after the first breeding record – nearly 100 pairs were nesting, spread through much of lowland England. By 1974 there were almost 500 pairs, and today little ringed plovers nest wherever there is suitable habitat, mostly in England but with a few pairs in Wales and the Scottish lowlands.

Little ringed plovers are summer visitors, spending the winters around the shores of the Mediterranean and through Africa. The males arrive back in Britain in late March and early April to be followed by the females through to the end of April and early May. Mating takes place immediately the pair come together, and the clutch of four eggs is laid, in a simple scrape in the gravel, in early May. About 25 days later the eggs hatch, and the young leave the nest as soon as their down is dry. After a further 24 days, the young fledge. Both eggs and young are very difficult to see, as they are so well camouflaged. It is essential, therefore, that the birds are not disturbed by people wandering across their nesting areas and perhaps accidentally trampling eggs or young.

Some pairs try to rear two broods in one year. Others that have lost their first clutch or brood will re-lay. By late June or early July, breeding is completed and the birds begin the first stage of their return migration to winter quarters. Initially, there seems to be something of a dispersal away from the nesting areas, so that in July one or more little ringed plovers may turn up almost anywhere there is freshwater with a muddy food-rich margin: by ponds and lakes, on salt-marsh saltpans, by farmland floodwaters, riversides, and so on.

There should be no problems with identification, though superficially this species bears some resemblance to its close relation, the ringed plover. The little ringed plover is noticeably smaller than the commoner ringed plover when the two are standing side by side. But the most conspicuous feature is the uniform, dark upper wing of the little ringed plover; the ringed plover has a white wing bar (this can be seen only when the birds are in flight, of course). The call is also diagnostic: a thin 'pee-u' in the little ringed plover that contrasts with the 'toooi' of the ringed plover. When the birds are watched closely on the ground, the putty-coloured legs and narrow yellow ring round the eye add a final confirmation.

Visit all your local gravel pits, sand pits, mining 'flashes' and areas of riverside shingle. Look out for little ringed plovers. If you see a pair do not disturb them. Send your observation to your county 'recorder'.

LITTLE RINGED PLOVER

Distribution

Key

▲ 1938   1967

1952   1990

Nest sites

It is interesting to note how many birds choose the best nest sites, when they have a choice. Take goldfinches, for example. They nest in trees and have a wide choice of places in the tree to build their nests: close to the main trunk where a branch forks out, in the fork of a major branch, near the top of the tree, or much lower down, and so on. However, the majority nest at the end of a horizontal or down-sloping branch, where the branch finally ends in a series of tiny twigs, and often very high (sometimes 60 ft from the ground). Here the nest is hidden from the eyes of avian predators by being immediately beneath the canopy of leaves, while the flimsy nature of the fine branches, together with the angle of the branches leading to the nest, makes it very difficult for ground predators to reach the eggs or nestlings. As far as the goldfinches are concerned, it is a perfect site.

Many species of sea birds are colonial nesters. In a colony they are more likely to repel predators than as widely scattered individuals. If one particular site is a good one, then it is better for many to share that site rather than the rest to be scattered on poorer sites. However, even colonial birds need their 'individual distance' and the nests are usually constructed just far enough apart to avoid adjacent pairs reaching each other from their nests. This means that, when the colony has outgrown the 'best' area for nest sites, other nests will be in a poorer place. Two examples of this are the black-headed gull and kittiwake.

In a salt-marsh black-headed gull colony that I studied, most gulls nested on slightly raised portions of the marsh, called 'levées'. These levées are narrow strips, alongside the main creeks, that are slightly higher than the surrounding marsh. There are two advantages of nesting on levées: by being a bit higher the birds have a good view across the salt-marsh and can see any predator approaching; during high spring tides the lower salt-marsh expanses may be flooded but the levées remain high and dry. I discovered that whereas over half of the eggs laid in nests on the raised levées hatched and nearly a third produced fledged young, only 8 per cent of eggs laid in nests on the lower marsh hatched – and none produced a fledged young.

Kittiwakes are cliff nesters, gluing their seaweed nests to narrow ledges with mud. In 1987 one small colony on Skomer Island had outgrown its usual ledges and rather than going further along the cliff to a new area, seven pairs built their nests on a short ledge just below the rest. Unfortunately, this ledge was below the maximum level reached by the highest tides. I watched them one day as the water level rose. They sat there, incubating their eggs, as slowly the tide reached them. They stood on their flooded nests and then retreated as their nests were washed away. Two days later they started to rebuild in the same place! Two weeks later they were washed out again!

Many birds remain faithful to one nest site for their entire reproductive life, and in some cases one nest site is used for several generations. A peregrine falcon eyrie in Longsleddale, Cumbria, has been used continuously since at least 1916.

Although to our eyes one bush is very much the same as another, one tree branch identical to the rest, one tussock of grass no different from the next one, and one cliff ledge just like another cliff ledge, to the birds that choose them as nest sites there are differences. One particular site seems better, often for reasons that are difficult for us to perceive, and that is chosen. In the case of the wren, it is the female who chooses the best site. The male makes several nests, all of which look good to him; but the eggs are laid in the one the female prefers.

Right A black-headed gull on the nest. Birds' nests are fascinating to find. But beware: you might unwittingly lead a predator to a nest by the trail of broken vegetation you leave. Do not disturb a nest without good reason.

Three woodland birds

Many people find it difficult to identify woodland birds because most such species are quite adept at disappearing rapidly with just a brief alarm call or spend most of the day flitting about in the tree tops. The problem is that 20th-century man has lost the ability to move quietly and slowly, and to notice the slightest movement, freeze instantly and then observe. So much will be missed by people who simply stroll through the wood and announce their presence to the woodland inhabitants by rustling their feet in the dead leaves or carelessly stepping on dry twigs. For the novice, the best way to watch woodland birds is not to go stamping around the wood, but to sit quietly with a tree as backrest, and to wait for the birds to come to you.

One of the most attractive of woodland birds is the nuthatch. Its patchy range is limited in the British Isles to England and Wales, and it is much commoner in the south and Midlands than the north, though it has been increasing in northern counties during recent years. It has two uniquely interesting behavioural features which careful observation will reveal. Nuthatches can run upwards, downwards and sideways on vertical tree trunks, unlike the woodpeckers and treecreeper, which can progress only in an upwards direction. Also, nuthatches nest in holes in trees (and nest boxes), but unlike other hole-nesters they reduce the entrance of the hole to the size that just permits them to pass through by cementing round it with mud.

Treecreepers are far more widespread than nuthatches, occurring wherever there are woodlands, parks and large gardens throughout the British Isles, with the exception of the Scottish islands. In spring, they are easily located by their thin, high-pitched song. But to watch one singing is rather more difficult because they often sing whilst climbing up a tree trunk, against which they are well camouflaged. A few clumsy strides towards the source of the song will usually be rewarded by the sight of a little brown bird disappearing into the distance! After the breeding season is over, treecreepers often join with parties of tits and goldcrests, roving through the higher branches. These mixed parties are worth locating, for with care and patience several woodland birds can be watched together. To watch a treecreeper running up a tree trunk like a little mouse, supporting itself with its stiff, pointed tail, and pecking under the bark for insects, requires ornithological skill.

One woodland species that is certainly overlooked more than most is the woodcock, for it is a secretive species with crepuscular habits, being most active at dusk and dawn. During the day, the woodcock lies quietly amongst undergrowth and relies on its remarkable camouflage to prevent it being discovered. Should it be disturbed, then it will fly away quickly through the trees, offering but a fleeting glimpse. However, from about March to the end of July woodcocks can be watched easily. At around dusk the male woodcock makes several circuits of its territory, known as 'roding flights', uttering a characteristic 'chiwick' call. It is a simple matter of sitting beneath one of these flight lines and watching the bird fly past, usually at tree-top height. Where woodcocks are especially numerous breeding birds, several may be watched simultaneously.

Woodcocks breed through much of the British Isles but are commonest in northern England and Scotland. There are areas where birds have not been recorded in the breeding season, such as parts of the West Country, West Wales and East Anglia, but sometimes the reason for this may be that they have been overlooked because of their secretive nature.

WOODCOCK

TREECREEPER

NUTHATCH

If you want to watch, instead of just see, nuthatches, treecreepers, woodcock and other fairly shy woodland birds then you must learn to be patient and quiet. A heavy approach will usually yield no more than a fleeting glimpse.

The lakeside in summer

Many birdwatchers consider July to be one of the worst months of the year. For most species the breeding season is over. The birds have stopped singing. Many of them are silent, moulting and secretive. The winter visitors are still on their northern breeding grounds, and autumn migration is only just starting. However, there is much to watch, provided an inquisitive attitude is adopted.

Every lake will have some of the commonest water birds, including mallard, coots, moorhens and perhaps a pair of mute swans and a family of dabchicks. These can provide a most interesting day, even in the 'dog-days' of high summer.

Mallard have a very long breeding season. Display and mating can occur as early as January and continue through to the end of June or even into July. So in July there will be mallard ducks with broods of ducklings ranging in age from just-hatched to fully-fledged. With a little patience and frequent visits, it is possible to get to know these broods quite intimately and follow their progress. July is also the main month for moult in the adult mallard and it is quite interesting to observe the rapid transition of the bright gaudy plumage of the drakes into the drab 'eclipse' plumage and then, through August and September, back into their new finery.

Coots have two and occasionally three broods in the course of the year. The first clutches are laid usually during late March and the young hatch and are on the water from the latter half of April. The last clutches are laid early in July and the young from these hatch in late July or early August. By contrast, moorhens have a somewhat longer breeding season

and often produce three broods, so that the adult moorhens are either incubating eggs or tending to their young from early March through to the end of October.

Get to know these common birds at the beginning of their breeding season. The easiest way to do this is to draw a large sketch map of your local lake and to note on it the territories of the coots and moorhens, and mute swans and grebes if these also occur. Female mallard may have their nests some distance from the lake, so you will have to wait until they arrive with their newly-hatched ducklings before you can get to know them. Then, as the young are taken on to the water, count the number in the brood and note that down with the date on your map. Mortality is high in broods of water birds, as large gulls, crows, rats, feral mink, foxes and even pike take their toll. So count each brood on every visit. Sometimes a brood will be missed one day because it is resting in a weedbed; but it may be found again on the next visit.

By July your map will be a mine of information and every visit will require much careful patient observation. For instance, a mallard duck that had three well-grown ducklings yesterday now has only two, but that other duck is either lucky or a very good mother for she has lost only one out of an initial brood of nine. And yet another duck has appeared with a brood of 11 tiny ducklings.

In that bay there are two large young coots feeding by themselves: they are the survivors of a brood of seven that was brought down to the water on 29 April. Their parents are a few yards away with a brood of five younger chicks; four days ago there were six so one has died or been killed.

Along that weedy margin close to the inflowing stream a pair of moorhens are feeding three tiny youngsters. What a season they have had! These are the first chicks they have brought to the water so presumably they have lost at least two clutches of eggs earlier, perhaps to rats from the stream.

Moorhen, coot and mallard are among the commonest breeding water birds on lakes. Many people dismiss them because they are 'always there', but a lot can be learnt by taking the time and trouble to watch them closely.

♀

♂

MALLARD

COOT

MOORHEN

Farmland gamebirds

Although pheasants are often seen feeding on open farmland, in the British Isles they are much more birds of woodland, especially woodlands that are carefully managed for the rearing and shooting of pheasants. By contrast, the red-legged partridge, common or grey partridge and quail are truly birds of the open fields, provided that (in the case of the partridges) there is suitable scrub or hedgerow cover for nesting.

Red-legged partridges are not native to these islands. They were first introduced as early as 1673 (this introduction failed), and then successfully from 1790 through to recent years. Most introductions were made to the vast cereal-growing areas of south-eastern England north to the Yorkshire Wolds and west to the Welsh Borders, but in recent years attempts have been made to extend their range to northern England, Scotland and the Isle of Man. Sometimes the red-legged partridge is referred to as the French partridge, signifying the origins of the eggs that were brought to this country.

Red-legged partridges were introduced to provide sport by supplementing the populations of the native grey partridge, for red-legs are generally much easier to raise in captivity than the native birds. However, on many estates they are not considered so worthy a quarry, for when 'beaten' they tend to run rather than fly and no game-shooter would dream of shooting at a running bird. For this reason, the remaining red-legs have often been left to fend for themselves with no further introductions to bolster the feral stock.

The grey partridge is far more widespread, occurring throughout England, southern and eastern Scotland, parts of Wales and central Ireland. However, the grey partridge has been declining over much of its range through the 20th century, with an especially marked decline since the 1960s. In some areas it continues to exist only because shooting pressure has been lessened and the wild stock has been supplemented by birds raised in captivity.

Several factors have led to the decline of the grey partridge. Cold springs followed by wet summers have possibly resulted in high chick mortality. The increasing use of pesticides on the arable fields has resulted in some partridges being poisoned and the decimation of the insects on which the young partridges feed. The ploughing and burning of stubbles in late summer and autumn has removed a significant amount of winter feeding. And in recent years there has been an agricultural trend to grub-up hedgerows to produce larger fields; this has removed nesting habitat and insect- and herb-rich feeding areas.

It may be that in years to come the grey partridge might become as rare as our third farmland gamebird, the quail, for this was a common bird in the British Isles through to the beginning of the 19th century. The quail is a summer visitor, arriving in late spring and departing during late September and October. Although most records of quail each year come from southern and central England and the Barrow and Liffey valleys of Ireland, they can occasionally be heard, if not seen, in most areas of extensive lowland grassland or cereal farmland. For some reason, there are sometimes 'good quail years' when they are reported throughout the British Isles.

The males have an unusual call that is generally described as 'wet-my-lips' and made from the middle of the growing vegetation, usually in the evening. However, it seems that they stop calling once breeding has commenced, so the fact that 'wet-my-lips' is no longer heard in a field where several male quail were calling a few days earlier may mean that they are breeding or have simply moved on.

COMMON
PARTRIDGE

♂

♀

RED-LEGGED
PARTRIDGE

♂

♀

QUAIL

Three contrasting game birds to look for on arable farmland are the resident grey partridge, the introduced red-legged partridge and the rarer quail.

Bird of the month: Avocet

The avocet has always been on the limits of its range in Britain, though it used to nest in colonies along the coast of England from the Humber south to Sussex. During the 18th and early 19th centuries numbers declined, and the last nested in Lincolnshire in 1837 and in Kent in 1842. Then, after a 96-year absence, two pairs arrived and remained to nest in 1938 in Co. Wexford in the Irish Republic. This proved to be a flash in the pan, for they never returned. However, in 1941 avocets returned to nest in England and they have continued to do so ever since.

In 1941 one pair nested in Norfolk, but their eggs were taken by an unscrupulous collector. Then in 1944 a pair nested in Essex and raised young. And again in Norfolk another pair nested in 1946, but once more the eggs were stolen. It was in 1947, when two sites in Suffolk were colonized, that the present story of the return of the avocet really began.

In that year, four pairs arrived at Minsmere and another four pairs at Havergate Island, ten miles away. The RSPB acted quickly to lease Minsmere and purchase Havergate. The following year, 1948, four pairs again arrived at Minsmere, but after displaying for a few days they left. Five pairs attempted to nest on Havergate and three or four pairs on nearby Lantern Marshes. Unfortunately, rats proved to be a major problem. Only three chicks were raised on Havergate and ten on Lantern Marshes. In 1949, after the draining of Lantern Island, all the avocets, together with a large colony of black-headed gulls, turned to Havergate, and 31 chicks were raised by 17 pairs. Careful management by the RSPB, including controlling the rat population, reinforcing the sea walls to prevent inundation by the spring tides, and regulating water levels so that there were always plenty of shallow-water feeding areas, paid dividends. Numbers grew steadily; and today more than 100 pairs nest each year on Havergate. Minsmere, which figured in the first year of the recolonization of Suffolk in 1947, was abandoned by avocets until 1963. Since then, avocets have nested there in increasing numbers, making this the second-largest colony in Britain. Since 1950, a few other pairs have attempted to breed elsewhere in East Anglia, Essex and Kent, suggesting that if there was more suitable habitat the species would be more widespread.

Avocets are summer visitors to their breeding colonies in northern Europe, moving southwards in winter to the Iberian Peninsula. However, a proportion of the British birds remain to winter in the estuaries of Devon and Cornwall, particularly the Tamar and Exe.

Striking in their plumage, call and behaviour, avocets are extremely selective as to their nesting and feeding requirements. Throughout Europe their most successful colonies are often closely associated with nesting terns and black-headed gulls, the latter possibly offering the avocets some protection from predators. They require feeding areas of very shallow, brackish water with rich supplies of tiny shrimps which they obtain by scything through the water with their curiously up-turned bills. Because such conditions are very localized in the British Isles, it is unlikely that the avocet will ever become a widespread breeding bird. And should a few pairs ever turn up somewhere, then their conspicuousness is likely to draw so much attention to them that they will be dissuaded from remaining to nest. In the 1970s, two pairs arrived in spring at one apparently suitable site in northern England. They displayed noisily. However, they eventually left because, almost certainly, too many birdwatchers and amateur bird photographers wanted a better view.

The RSPB has the avocet as its emblem because it was one of the first of many species that would now probably be extinct in the British Isles but for the Society's efforts.

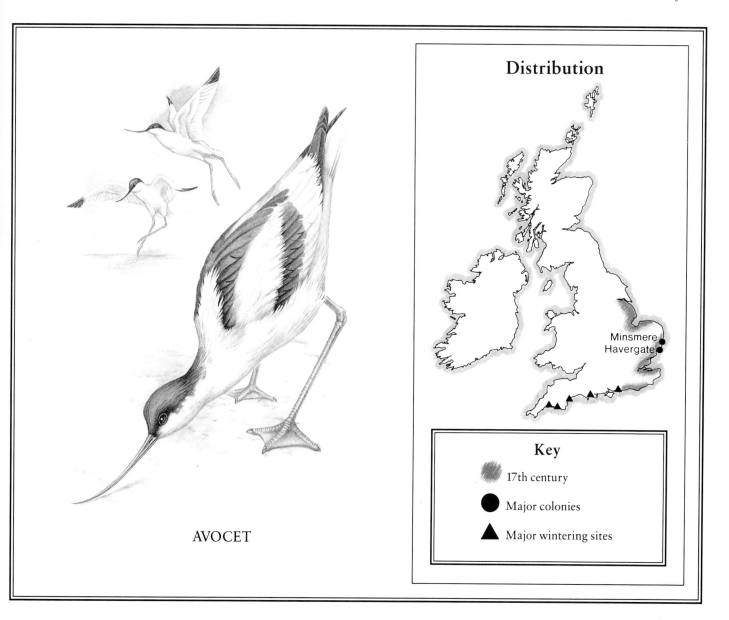

Distribution

Minsmere
Havergate

AVOCET

Key

17th century

Major colonies

Major wintering sites

Moulting

One of the problems in having a feather plumage is that the feathers become worn even though they are carefully preened and oiled each day. Worn feathers are less efficient conservers of heat; worn flight feathers result in less efficient flight. So birds must shed their feathers when they become worn and replace them with new ones, a process known as moulting.

Moulting is energy-demanding, so the birds need extra food supplies. At the same time, when feathers have been shed and new ones are in the process of growth, flight and heat conservation are less effective. It is not surprising, therefore, that the periods of moult are also periods of high mortality in bird populations.

The process of moult is rather like the replacement of milk-teeth by permanent teeth in humans. The old feathers are replaced with the new ones a few at a time. And the old feather is lost as the new feather pushes outwards and displaces it. Thus, as several feathers are shed, so their replacements grow out from the same feather follicles. The replacement of the feathers in this way is carried out in a fairly orderly fashion.

This pattern of moult is most easily seen in the secondary and primary flight feathers. In most species, the long primary feathers are shed in turn from the innermost ones outwards, whilst the secondaries are shed in turn from the outermost (those in the middle of the wing, close to the primaries) towards the body. This can be clearly seen in larger birds, such as waders and gulls, in late summer. As they fly past, a noticeable gap can be seen in the middle of the wing of birds that have just begun their moult where the adjacent outermost secondaries and innermost primaries have been shed. The pattern is not universal, however, for in the spotted flycatcher the primary feathers are moulted beginning with the outermost feathers.

The situation in wildfowl is again quite different. In these, all the flight feathers are moulted simultaneously, which means that there is a period of several days in which all ducks, geese and swans are flightless. The birds are extremely vulnerable to predation at this time, so the gaudy plumage of the drake mallard and teal is replaced by a dingy 'eclipse' plumage that provides some camouflage, and the birds become very secretive, hiding away in rushes and reedbeds.

In most species the body feathers are moulted twice each year and the flight feathers just once. This means that many species can have a quite different winter and summer plumage. In this way a drab winter plumage, which camouflages the bird in its winter quarters, may be replaced in spring by a gaudier summer plumage that is used in display. And then the breeding plumage is shed in autumn for the drab winter plumage. In their first year of life, most birds have one extra moult of the body feathers. The first plumage of soft down is replaced by a juvenile plumage with which the bird fledges. Then, during the autumn or early winter, the juvenile plumage is replaced by a winter plumage; and in spring a further moult occurs to give the bird a summer plumage.

In several species, such as the eagles, gannet and gulls, it may take a bird three or more years before it is sexually mature. In these there is a sequence of plumages that the bird progresses through at each moult before it has its full adult plumage. Because the timing of the annual moults is quite distinct, it is possible to calculate precisely the ages of immature gannets and great black-backed gulls, provided the plumage sequences are known.

Right *The pied wagtail in three different stages of plumage: adult summer, adult winter, and juvenile. Feathers become worn, and so all birds must replace them at least once in the course of the year.*

Family ties

After the nesting season is over, the fledged young of many species remain with their parents for some time. This is most obvious in larger species. For instance, everyone has seen a pair of mute swans still with their fully-grown cygnets in autumn and early winter. Throughout August, pairs of carrion crows can be seen feeding with their young on the moor, while on the shore pairs of black-headed gulls will be pestered for food by their brown-and-white off-spring. Young blackbirds and starlings often perch on the garden fence, squawking, as they wait for their parents to bring them more earthworms. And in the reeds a duck mallard will be resting with her brood of four fully-grown ducklings, while on the open water a family of coots will be diving for waterweeds.

The nesting season of the tree sparrow finishes usually in early August. If they have been especially successful, a pair may have had two broods and raised a total of about 12 young to fledging. By the time the second brood has left the nest, the first brood may be quite independent: they will have been fledged for about six weeks. However, they tend to keep fairly close to the nest site in their parents' territory while the second brood is being reared. Then both broods and parents usually collect together and remain in one tightly-knit group into the autumn.

By August, most goldfinches have completed nesting and the family parties then roam the country-side in search of food. One of the traditional favourite foods of goldfinches in autumn is the thistle head. Large areas of scrub or waste ground that have thick stands of thistles are eagerly sought by the goldfinch family parties. And because nesting territories have broken down, several families may feed together in the one thistle patch. Sometimes several families will join together into a large goldfinch 'charm'.

Some pairs of linnets have three broods during one year, so that it is sometimes not until August and occasionally early September before their third brood is fledged. From then through the autumn and winter, the parent linnets and all their young roam farm-lands, hedgerows, waste ground and larger gardens in search of seeds. Several family parties of linnets may unite to produce flocks of over 100 birds.

As autumn progresses, many species of finches and sparrows join together in large flocks. Usually similar species of birds have different foods to reduce competition between them, but in the abundance of the natural harvest of autumn, these dietary differ-ences sometimes disappear. On estuarine rice-grass marshes, it is possible to watch a mixed flock of green finches, chaffinches, linnets, house sparrows and tree sparrows feeding together as though they were all members of the same species, while on the moorland edge of the central Pennines, mixed flocks of linnets and twites often occur together, feeding on grass seeds and sedge fruits. And on stubbles close to a lakeside, a mixed flock of chaffinches, linnets, tree sparrows, yellowhammers and reed buntings may all be feeding together on grain spilt at harvest.

Why family parties, and why flocks? The main problem facing young birds is that of finding food. By keeping together in family parties, the experienced adults can lead their fledged young to good feeding areas. If the young were to separate from their parents as soon as they fledged, they might not be able to find sufficient food resources and could die.

Secondly, by feeding in family parties or, perhaps even better, in flocks consisting of many family parties and sometimes several species, there is more chance of an approaching predator being noticed. Most birds may be intent on feeding, but at least one might be on the alert.

LINNET

♀

♂

TREE SPARROW

GOLDFINCH

After the breeding season look out for family parties of species like the goldfinch, linnet and tree sparrow. In your diary record the number in the group, where they were and what they were feeding on.

Exodus from the dales

One of the ornithological highlights of the dales of northern England and Scotland is the wealth of their breeding wader populations. By the river are common sandpipers and oystercatchers, while in the riverside fields are lapwings, redshanks and curlews. And on the surrounding hills, dunlins and golden plovers will be found. For so many people, the wild calls of these birds are almost synonymous with the dales and uplands. However, all these waders come here for one purpose only – to nest and raise their young to fledging. And then, as soon as they can, they leave the dales.

Throughout the winter they are elsewhere, on the shores and mild coastal plains and farmlands of the lowlands, or, in the case of the common sandpiper, in tropical Africa. They return to the dales in early spring. Often a day spent in Airedale in early March will be notable for the lack of lapwings, redshanks, oystercatchers and curlews. But that evening the silence of the still air will be broken with their calls as they fly overhead. The next day, oystercatchers will be resting on riverside shingle, curlews and redshanks will be probing and pecking the wet pastures for food, and a small flock of lapwings will be sleeping in the meadow.

Then, through April and May they separate, form territories, display and mate, and lay their eggs. Come June, most of them have young. Golden plovers will pipe plaintively and dunlins trill quietly to warn their chicks as you approach across the moor. Lapwings, curlews and redshanks will shout in annoyance as you walk across their fields. By the river, common sandpipers will utter 'tweedle-deee' to tell their chicks to remain hidden. And oystercatchers will carry out their ridiculous distraction display by running away with head down and then pretend that they are sitting on a nest hundreds of yards away from where you know the chicks are hiding.

In only three or four months these waders complete their breeding cycle, so that by July or early August they can leave with their young. Their departure occurs usually on warm, still, clear evenings, usually in a westerly or south-westerly direction, towards the Irish Sea. From the edge of the moor there is a constant stream overhead of dunlins and golden plovers, and of oystercatchers, redshanks, curlews and lapwings along the valley. Soon they have all left. This is a sad time for dalesfolk, for though it is still summer, the valleys are now silent.

However, we can follow these waders. In the towns and cities of north-west England and the central lowlands of Scotland, they may be heard calling after sunset as they continue their journey to the estuaries and coastal farmlands of the Solway, Morecambe Bay, Ribble, Dee and Severn. The young birds have never made this journey before so perhaps the constant calls of their parents help the families keep together on this short migration.

For those birdwatchers on the estuaries, the arrival of these birds that have bred not too far away is a welcome sight, for it marks the beginning of the autumn migration. As the exodus from the dales continues, so the number of common sandpipers feeding along the edges of the salt-marsh creeks increases. In Morecambe Bay and on the Solway, the flocks of oystercatchers, curlews and redshanks may soon total many thousands on the mudflats and mussel scaups. By the Ribble, Dee and Severn, the flocks of lapwings and golden plovers on the wet pastures grow quickly, while on the Mersey mudflats parties of dunlins feed keenly, the adults still with some trace of their moorland nesting plumage and their young in juvenile dress.

Among the earliest of the migrations is that of the birds that breed in the uplands and winter on the coast. During late July and through August it is possible in some regions to watch species like the oystercatcher, lapwing, golden plover and redshank making their exodus to winter quarters.

REDSHANK

LAPWING

♂

♀

OYSTERCATCHER

GOLDEN
PLOVER

Autumn sea-bird movements

Sea-bird migrations are often easy and exciting to watch, especially in autumn. Some points need to be stressed first, however. The choice of site is very important: pick a point or promontory that will enable you to see birds that are passing within range of most parts of the coast. Places like Fife Ness, Emanuel Head on Lindisfarne, Spurn, Blakeney Point, Dungeness, Hartland Point and Formby Point are ideal. Find a suitable position about 20 ft above the sea. Unless you have a telescope, you must be prepared to miss many birds that will pass out of range of binoculars. The best time to make observations is usually when there is a strong onshore wind that brings the birds that bit closer to the coast.

Two commoner birds that are worth watching and counting as they pass by are the herring and lesser black-backed gulls. Herring gulls are fairly sedentary birds; they do not migrate in the sense that most lesser black-backed gulls migrate to the Bay of Biscay and north-west Africa for the winter. So on a long sea-watch, beginning at low water and continuing through high water and on to the next low water (a gruelling session of over 12 hours), an interesting pattern may emerge:

	Lesser black-backs		Herring gulls	
Flight direction	North	South	North	South
Up to high water	14	1276	51	243
After high water	31	572	301	40

What we have recorded here, from a late-August sea-watch, is the migration southwards of lots of lesser black-backed gulls throughout the day, as well as some general movements to and fro of a few lesser black-backs and good numbers of herring gulls on the tide. The herring gulls recorded heading south before high water were moving to roost and then, when the tide ebbed, they moved back to their low-water feeding areas.

Sea-watching enables many scarce or local British breeding species to be seen around the entire coast. For example, the little tern is now quite a rare nesting bird. However, in autumn they can be seen passing southwards on their way back to the tropical coasts of Africa. As their name suggests, they are very small birds and are easily overlooked as they pass low over the sea, often hidden momentarily in the wave troughs. So it is also worth checking harbours, sandy bays and estuaries in autumn, for all terns stop off to feed in these habitats during their migration.

To see skuas on their breeding grounds one usually has to travel to the north of Scotland. However, in autumn they migrate through the North Sea and English Channel, through the Irish Sea or around the west coast of Ireland. Stiff winds will often bring them close inshore and make skuas the highlight of many a sea-watch. On the east coast of England and Scotland, some quite large numbers may be noted. In one six-hour watch 324 arctic skuas, 41 bonxies and two pomarine skuas passed south at Fife Ness. Off Lancashire's Formby Point, 11 arctic skuas, three bonxies and single pomarine and long-tailed skuas passed during a gale in four hours: all four European skuas in one day!

Skuas are piratical birds, waylaying lesser sea birds to force them to give up their food. Migrating terns and kittiwakes are often pursed by arctic skuas. Bonxies have been observed to bully the larger gannets into disgorging their stomach contents. Bonxies will go even further, having been known to kill and devour young kittiwakes and black-headed gulls during their autumn migration.

A sea-watch from a coastal headland in autumn may be rewarded with the spectacle of many commoner sea birds, like the herring and lesser black-backed gulls, passing offshore. Among them may be scarcer species, like the bonxie (or great skua) and little tern, and in a gale even rarer birds, such as the sooty shearwater and pomarine skua, may pass close by.

LITTLE TERN

GREAT SKUA

LESSER BLACK-BACKED
GULL

HERRING GULL

Bird of the month: Red kite

The red kite was once a well-known, common and widespread bird throughout Britain, though there is no evidence that it ever nested in Ireland. It was certainly a familiar bird up to the end of the 18th century in towns and cities, where it scavenged for a living on the rubbish that was thrown out into the streets. And perhaps it was an improvement in sanitation that brought about the first stage of a rapid decline in kite numbers. In the 18th century, wealthy landowners began to run their estates as preserves for the sport of shooting where game might breed, free from interference from human poachers and carnivorous mammals and birds. One job of the 'gamekeeper' was to exterminate ruthlessly anyone or any animal that might cause the loss of even a single gamebird or mammal. In many areas, a bounty was even paid for the corpses of species like polecats, pine martens, foxes, eagles, harriers and kites.

By the middle of the 19th century, kites were becoming scarce, and collecting scarce things was a popular Victorian pursuit. So the remaining kites and their nests were eagerly sought for collections. By about 1890, the species had ceased to breed regularly in Scotland, though there is a record of a nest in Glen Garry in 1917. In England, the kite last nested in Lincolnshire – once a stronghold of the species – in 1870, and by 1880 it had gone from the West Midlands and counties bordering Wales. In 1913 the last pair in England attempted to rear young in a wooded Devon valley, but failed.

Only in central Wales did the kite survive, though in very small numbers. This area, centred on the cwms and sheep-walks in the upper Ystwyth, Teifi, Tywi and Elan Valleys, is primarily sheep pasture. Kites feed to a large extent on carrion, especially dead sheep. And many hill farmers who saw kites feeding on dead lambs assumed, quite wrongly, that the kites had killed the lambs. So even here the kites were persecuted by shooting, trapping and by poisoning with animal corpses baited with strychnine. It was only because a few naturalists, including the infant RSPB, spent a great deal of time and money protecting them that there were any kites left in 1954, when the first major Bird Protection Act was passed by Parliament. Though this Welsh population had been as low as just three pairs in some years, Col. H. M. Salmon, one of the leading protectors, recounted that in 1954 there were 15 pairs of kites, 12 of which reared just 15 young, and that at the end of the season the total population was 55 individuals.

Despite some continuing persecution by gamekeepers and hill farmers, losses in the 1950s and 1960s due to poisoning with organo-chloride pesticides, and the barbaric 'hobby' of egg collecting – which have continued to this day – the numbers of Welsh kites have gradually increased. Yet, without the hard work each year still being done by the Nature Conservancy and RSPB, the situation might easily be reversed. Keen birdwatchers who want to see our native kites should do so without making the job of those guarding them more difficult.

Welsh kites are very easy to locate by driving along the maze of country lanes that dissect their range in central Wales and keeping a careful look-out for them flying overhead. Then it is simply a matter of parking the car and enjoying the spectacle from the roadside. With a little perseverance, you might be lucky enough to watch them feeding on the remains of a dead sheep with buzzards and ravens. In the evening, you may even be fortunate enough to find one of their communal roosts and enjoy the sight of a number of kites indulging in aerial acrobatics over a hillside oak wood.

Once common through much of Britain, the red kite was brought to the verge of extinction. Today only a small population remains, in central Wales.

RED KITE

Distribution

Key

The number of reports of red kites is increasing throughout Britain, away from their Welsh strongholds. Should this trend continue and the birds enjoy adequate protection, the red kite might soon return to breed in several of its 19th-century sites.

Mortality

Suppose that a pair of robins have two nests in one year, lay five eggs in each and raise all ten young to fledging. Suppose, too, that all ten young and both adults survive to the following breeding season. And suppose that every pair of robins did the same. There would then be six pairs of robins where there had been just one. On the face of it, this might be an attractive prospect, for the robin is a very beautiful and popular bird. But the result would be catastrophic, especially if such a utopian situation prevailed over several years. The birds might outstrip their food supply, resulting in mass starvation. There would be insufficient territories so huge numbers would roam the countryside seeking somewhere to stay; but wherever they went, the resident territory holders would simply move them on. No! The ideal for our commoner birds is to have a reproductive output that replaces the older birds that die, and maintains a constant population. This means that a large proportion of the eggs laid in one year must not produce adult birds or, to put it another way, that each pair of birds raise just two young to adulthood in their lives, to replace themselves.

This means, of course, that many young birds must die before they reach adulthood. That this is the case can be seen from a 'life table' for blackbirds calculated from a study carried out in the 1980s: 100 eggs laid = 36 young hatch = 12 young fledge = 1.4 young reach the age of one year and breed. The figure of 1.4 blackbirds entering the breeding population replaced those adults that had died, so the population over six years remained almost constant.

However, on occasion the normal population regulation system is overridden by catastrophe. Mortality increases suddenly and rapidly. Since the 1920s, the dumping of waste crude oil at sea by oil tankers and 'accidents' like the *Torrey Canyon* have increased the mortality rates of guillemots to such an extent that the birth rate was greatly outstripped and the population crashed. During the 1950s and early 1960s, deaths attributable to poisoning by DDT and other organo-chlorine agricultural insecticides were so great that the populations of sparrowhawks, merlins, golden eagles and peregrines fell alarmingly. And during the 1947 and 1962–63 arctic winter weather, the populations of species such as the heron, kingfisher and wren were decimated.

In the subsequent series of mild winters, though, herons, kingfishers and wrens have had higher breeding success rates than mortality rates and their populations have recovered. And following the ban on the use of persistent pesticides, the populations of birds of prey have similarly recovered. But despite a ban on tankers flushing crude oil into the seas around the coasts of the British Isles, illicit spilling continues and 'accidents' occur with the consequence that the guillemot population has not yet recovered.

But it is clear that when a catastrophe (whether natural or man-made) is brought to an end, bird populations may recover quite quickly providing there are enough of them remaining to make a viable breeding stock. The reduced population can have large territories in the best habitat; competition between birds for territories and food will be minimal; food will be abundant. So mortality will be low and the reproductive output high. But once the population has reached the level that can be sustained by the habitat, mortality rates will rise to maintain a constant population.

There is thus a rule worth remembering when birds are found dead or dying: where the population density is high, so too is mortality; where the population is low, then mortality is low.

Right *A seabird killed by crude oil spillage. Natural and man-made causes take a heavy toll of young birds: the rate of mortality is higher in the first six months of life than in all subsequent six-month periods.*

SEPTEMBER

'Little brown jobs'

Many birdwatchers, especially those who have only just taken up the hobby, find the identification of warblers very difficult, particularly birds on autumn migration when they skulk in dense undergrowth or, when flushed, flit from one bush into another. Often a birdwatcher will be seen walking from bush to bush, and back again, glaring through the binoculars. And when questioned about what has been found, the answer will frequently be: 'Oh! A little brown job! It might be a ... warbler!'

The situation is even worse, and often quite amusing, at one of the bird observatories when a scarce or rare warbler appears on an autumn Friday. At dawn the following day, several coach parties and scores of cars will arrive, crammed with birdwatchers, binoculars and telescopes. When, at Spurn, a Radde's warbler and several yellow-browed warblers had appeared during the week, the road to the observatory was solid with cars on Saturday.

Soon a crowd of over 100 were straining their eyes to catch a glimpse of a little brown job that was flitting nervously about in a hawthorn hedge. All were convinced that this was a yellow-browed warbler, for one had been seen there two days earlier. It was pointed out to them that this bird was, in fact, a garden warbler and that if they looked further along the hedge there was a red-breasted flycatcher – and if they looked in the hedge behind them, *there* was a yellow-browed. The crowd split instantly as both rare birds were chased quickly into thicker cover.

Unfortunately, the illustrations of warblers given in books are of birds seen under the most perfect of conditions at close range. Look at the examples shown here. The darkish head accentuates the diagnostic pale superciliary eye-stripe of the sedge warbler, the back and mantle are well streaked, and the rump is a uniform rufous colour. The overall brown-streaked plumage of the grasshopper warbler is also quite characteristic. And the nondescript browns of the reed warbler allow for easy identification, if the very similar but rare marsh, paddyfield and Blythe's reed warblers are discounted!

But now stick these pictures into the middle of a clump of sea buckthorn or a patch of brambles, on an overcast day with drizzle. And just before you get the binoculars focused on one, have somebody take it away immediately. It is not so easy now!

Several things are required to enjoy finding and identifying drab, skulking warblers. The first is stealth and silence: what use is a view of the rear of the bird as it enters the next bush? The second is patience. By sitting down and waiting, a little brown job that you have discovered will eventually emerge from cover and give you good views. The third is a pair of good binoculars that will help you see the bird in focus immediately it emerges. High-powered instruments, with a magnification of ten or more, are perfect for open spaces, but at close range in cover they are not as good as a pair with a magnification of seven or eight. For this reason, some expert birdwatchers carry two pairs of binoculars. The fourth requirement is knowing what you are looking for, or knowing the range of bird species that you little brown job might belong to. And the fifth is ensuring that you are with no more than two other observers.

Finally do not believe all those who go around in crowds and boast that they have seen lanceolated, Pallas's grasshopper, paddyfield, booted, dusky and arctic warblers. What they really mean is that they were there when a little brown job disappeared from view amongst some undergrowth and which they were told was a ... warbler. Or that the warden showed them one in the hand that he had just caught.

GRASSHOPPER
WARBLER

REED WARBLER

SEDGE WARBLER

Perhaps the most difficult group of birds to identify in autumn are the warblers: the 'little brown jobs'. How do you identify a little brownish bird that is skulking in the bottom of a bush? The answer is patience and knowing what to look for.

What is our commonest bird?

If I were to ask you what you think our commonest bird is, perhaps even choosing two species, what would your answer be, I wonder?

It is indeed a very difficult question to answer, as you may have just discovered. It is tempting to think immediately of a bird that we encounter frequently and in large numbers. The starling or house sparrow, perhaps. But then we might remember that most of the British Isles does not consist of back-gardens and town parks. There are vast areas of mountain and moorland where house sparrows and starlings are very thin on the ground. Possibly we ought to consider a species that occurs in high densities from almost the tops of the highest mountains to the rough grasslands of coastal dunes and salt-marshes: the meadow pipit. But what about the skylark? For although this is not as numerous as the meadow pipit on the higher moorlands, it is far more abundant on the lowland pastures and meadows.

It is now clear that there are two factors to be taken into account when trying to find the answer to this question:

Commonness = abundance and distribution

At the end of the 19th century and beginning of the 20th century, it is possible that a sea bird, the puffin, was the most abundant British bird. One colony, St Kilda, was estimated as having up to 3 million birds. Ailsa Craig had 'immense numbers', as also did islands off Skye, North Rona, the Shiants, the Isles of Scilly and Great Saltee. Ronald Lockley reported that, in 1890, Grassholm, off the Pembrokeshire coast, had half a million birds. And there were many smaller colonies that held hundreds and thousands of birds. This situation has changed, though, for the puffin population has crashed dramatically in the 20th century. But even when the puffin was perhaps the most abundant British bird, it was not the commonest, for it was by no means widespread.

From my own researches and a thorough search of the ornithological literature, the most abundant species seem to be as follows:

1. Wren – 10 million pairs*
2. Blackbird – 7 million pairs
3. Chaffinch – 6¼ million pairs
4. Blue tit – 5¼ million pairs
5. Robin – 5 million pairs
6. Dunnock – 4½ million pairs
7. {Woodpigeon / House sparrow** / Skylark} 4 million pairs
8. {Song thrush / Meadow pipit} 3½ million pairs

*Following very hard winters, the populations of wrens and song thrushes may be much lower.
**The house sparrow population is certainly much less than the 7 million pairs estimated several years ago. The starling, too, would have just figured in this list 20 years ago, but it also seems to have declined and now has a population of about 3 million pairs.

Distribution is the last factor to be considered. Only one bird on this list occurs from the Shetlands and Outer Hebrides to the far west of Ireland and southernmost corners of England. It is also the only one to nest in the most mountainous of uplands and on precipitous sea cliffs, as well as in lowland farmland, woodland, scrub, suburban gardens and parks in the centres of our cities. The wren. Thus, because it has the greatest geographical distribution and occurs in the widest range of habitats, it is the most widespread of our birds.

The wren is our most numerous breeding bird and the most widespread. It is therefore the commonest bird of the British Isles.

Four common birds. But which is Britain's commonest?

BLACKBIRD

♀ ♂

BLUE TIT

SONG THRUSH

♀ ♂

CHAFFINCH

Autumn wader migration

The estuaries and bays of the British Isles are important staging posts for about 3 million waders that breed in Greenland, Iceland, Scandinavia and Siberia. Many pass through in autumn on their way to destinations in Africa and the Iberian Peninsula, but some remain for the winter.

There are two identifiable subspecies of black-tailed godwits in western Europe. The one that breeds in eastern Europe and the Low Countries is quite a dingy affair in its breeding plumage compared with the dark red-brown Icelandic variety. But although a few European black-tailed godwits do breed on wet grasslands in south-eastern England, most of those that pass through or winter in the British Isles are of the Icelandic race. They begin to arrive back on British estuaries in July, with numbers rapidly accumulating to peak in late August or September. Many then move on, further south.

When they arrive in autumn, most adult black-tailed godwits are still in their breeding plumage, and it is not until mid-September that they have completed their moult into their grey winter plumage.

All the bar-tailed godwits that arrive on British shores in autumn are from breeding grounds in northern Scandinavia and the USSR. So in the breeding season there is a distinct geographical separation of black- and bar-tailed godwits. This separation continues on our estuaries. Black-tailed godwits feed almost exclusively on the ooziest of mudflats where they use their long bills to probe for tiny ragworms, while bar-tailed godwits frequent the sandier shores where they take small molluscs from just beneath the surface of the beach or probe at the water's edge for lugworms. Even where they occur on the same estuary, their paths rarely cross, for the black-tailed godwit usually has its high-water roost further up the estuary, close to its muddy feeding grounds, whereas the bar-tailed godwit roosts in the outer estuary closer to its sandier feeding grounds. This is a perfect example of ecological separation between two very similar species so that both can co-exist without competition.

The dunlin is the most widespread of the world's waders, breeding in the Arctic and subarctic regions of North America (where it is known as the red-backed sandpiper), in Greenland and Iceland, on the moors and marshes of northern Britain and Ireland, and through Scandinavia and Siberia. With such a huge range, it is not surprising that ornithologists recognize several distinct races. At least three regularly pass through, or winter in, estuaries of the British Isles: the race *Calidris alpina schinzii* that breeds in Britain and southern Scandinavia, the race *C. a. alpina* that breeds in northern Scandinavia and western Siberia, and the race *C. a. arctica* that breeds in Greenland. Unfortunately, these races cannot be identified without catching the birds, with the possible exception of *C. a. alpina*, which has a much longer bill than the other two. Our knowledge of the wide origins of the dunlins, and other waders, that pass through the British Isles comes from very intensive studies carried out here and abroad in recent years by dedicated ornithologists.

There are currently under consideration plans to develop many of our bays and estuaries – to make these vast 'unprofitable' areas more 'profitable'. If all these plans were to be carried out in the next decade, the wader habitats of the Solway, Duddon, Morecambe Bay, Ribble, Mersey, Dee, Severn, Wash, and so on, will have been obliterated. With nowhere to stop and feed on their autumn migrations, these huge wader populations will have also been obliterated by the next millenium.

DUNLIN

BAR-TAILED
GODWIT

BLACK-TAILED
GODWIT

Black-tailed godwits from Iceland, bar-tailed godwits from Siberia, and dunlins from northern Britain, Scandinavia, Siberia and Greenland are among the huge number of waders that pass through our estuaries and bays in autumn.

Bird of the month: Bearded reedling

Bearded reedlings (or bearded tits as they are also commonly called) are birds of extensive reedbeds. Up to the 19th century, when development of much of the British countryside reached a climax, they were quite widespread in south-eastern Britain from Lincolnshire through East Anglia and on south to Kent and west to Hampshire. However, drainage of much of the region's wetlands resulted in destruction of habitat and a consequent contraction of their range. By the beginning of the 20th century, the remaining population was centred on the Norfolk Broads, with only a few pairs elsewhere.

Bearded reedlings are amongst the most susceptible species of birds to hard winters. The problem is not so much the cold but the inability of the birds to feed on reed heads that are covered with a glazing of ice or snow. Studies published by the British Trust for Ornithology have shown that the winters of 1916–17, 1939–40 and 1962–63 were particularly hard. After the latter, it has been recorded that only a single male was reported from the Norfolk population and that only a few pairs remained in Suffolk. That particular harsh winter affected also the Dutch population; it fell from many thousands of pairs to barely 100 pairs.

After 1963, the populations of both Holland and England recovered rapidly, and for the first time 'eruptive behaviour' was noted in the bearded reedling. This behaviour occurs in areas of high population density and carries surplus birds away to either colonize new areas or die. It is well-known trait in species such as the waxwing, in which every few years the population of the USSR builds up and then erupts, with large numbers of birds heading westwards, many of them crossing the North Sea and reaching Britain. Eruption of the bearded reedling occurs in September and October. Parties of birds may be seen leaving the reeds and flying high into the air. Often they return to their reedbed, but occasionally a party will continue to gain ascent and fly off.

Many bearded reedlings that were ringed in Holland have been recovered, following eruption, at British sites where bearded reedlings have never before been recorded: places like Hornsea Mere in Humberside and Shotton Pools by the Welsh Dee, Clwyd. During one of the earliest eruptions, in 1965, a party of nine was observed flying northwards along the Lancashire coast between Liverpool and Southport – the first record for this county – and by early November bearded reedlings had arrived at the large reedbed RSPB reserve at Leighton Moss. Since then, Leighton Moss has been a breeding stronghold of the species in the north-west of England, a region that did not have bearded reedlings in earlier times.

Through the autumn, it is extremely worthwhile visiting reedbeds that may never before have had bearded reedlings recorded there. Sooner or later, a party that has erupted from one of the main breeding concentrations will turn up. They are easily located by their characteristic, nasal, explosive 'ping-ping' call notes, which are used as contact calls to keep the foraging flock in touch with each other in the dense reed stands. Then it is a matter of waiting patiently for them to appear at the edge of the reeds or amongst the reed seed heads. There may be an adult male, recognized by its characteristic lavender-grey head and black moustache (hardly a beard!), amongst them, but most will be immature birds with a predominantly brown-and-buff plumage and a very long tail. The birds may remain the entire winter; who knows, they may even remain to breed. And then, when numbers have grown, in future autumns they may be seen erupting from there, possibly to colonize yet another reedbed.

The bearded reedling rarely occurs away from reedbeds. Although the British population is centred on the fens of East Anglia, reedlings might appear in autumn in any reed area after an 'eruption'.

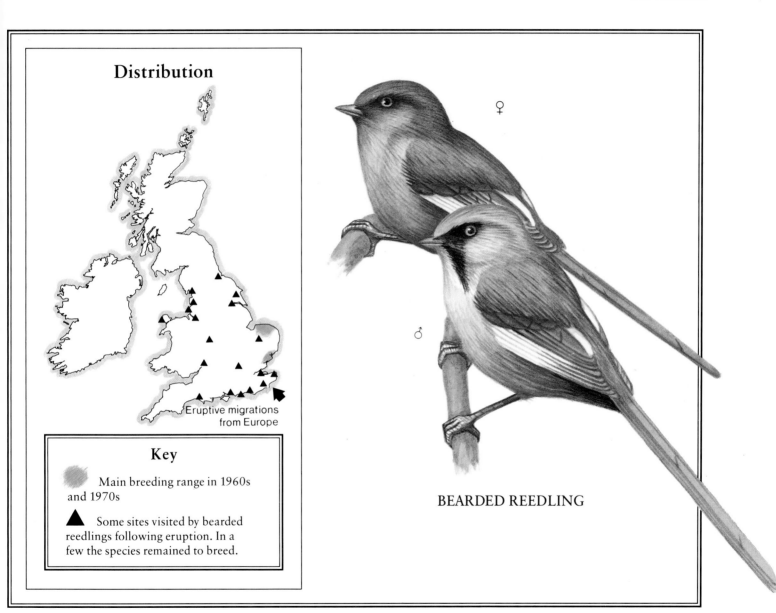

Distribution

Eruptive migrations
from Europe

Key

Main breeding range in 1960s
and 1970s

Some sites visited by bearded
reedlings following eruption. In a
few the species remained to breed.

♀

♂

BEARDED REEDLING

Autumn migration

Every autumn, millions of birds that have bred or been born in the British Isles head southwards. These are the summer visitors that winter as far afield as southern Africa and the South Atlantic. At the same time, millions of birds that have spent the summer breeding in Scandinavia, Siberia, Iceland and Greenland stream southwards to spend the winter in the British Isles: our winter visitors. Many other birds, which have neither bred in the British Isles nor will winter here, pass through. These passage migrants may stay here for a few days to refuel before continuing their southwards journey.

The comings and goings of autumn migrants are not as easy to observe as are the arrivals of the first swallows, willow warblers and cuckoos in spring. The reason for this is that the birds arrive in spring in quite distinct waves, as if there was some urgency in the matter. And there is; they are rushing to gain nesting territories under the influence of a sexual urge. By contrast, in autumn the migration of a particular species is spread over a long period. Thus, some willow warblers begin their return migration as early as July whilst others are still leaving in October.

Autumn migration can be readily observed. Or at least, evidence of migration can be gathered, for it is very difficult to watch many species migrating because they travel under cover of darkness. On clear nights, the 'seep-seep' calls of migrating redwings may be heard high overhead as they arrive from Iceland or Scandinavia. Several hours spent gazing through a telescope at the face of the full moon may be rewarded with a view of nocturnal migrants winging their way southwards. The easiest way of witnessing migration, however, is to spend a week's holiday in one of the major bird observatories. Spurn Head on the Humberside coast is one of the greatest of these observatories.

For the first two or three days the weather may not have been conducive to migration on a big scale, with strong westerly winds and rain. But then in the evening the winds veer round to the north-east and the skies clear over the North Sea. Bed early! An early cup of tea in the Warren Cottage and you step out in the first glimmer of dawn. The buckthorn bushes are alive with migrants that have just completed their journey across the North Sea and are busily searching for food. As you stroll down the concrete track leading along Spurn Head, the torch picks out some birds that are exhausted and resting on the ground. Soon it is light enough to use the binoculars. There are scores of pied and spotted flycatchers and redstarts. Willow warblers, whitethroats, lesser whitethroats and garden warblers flit from bush to bush. Blackbirds, song thrushes, redwings, fieldfares and one or two ring ouzels are guzzling down vast quantities of the red buckthorn berries. You spend some time watching a bluethroat and a couple of wrynecks. Somebody shouts: 'They have caught a yellow-browed warbler in one of the ringing traps!' You rush to examine it before it is released. There are birds everywhere!

You walk down to Narrow Neck. Suddenly there is a rush of wings as a flock of thrushes descends vertically to make their landfall. You look out over the sea and notice a speck of a bird flying towards you: you are witnessing a solitary woodcock completing its long journey from Norway. Suddenly swallows start streaming southwards: they migrate during the day. Hundreds of terns fly slowly southwards offshore. Occasionally an arctic skua or a bonxie breaks its southward progress to persecute one of them into disgorging its last meal. Terns and skuas also migrate by day. That is migration!

Right Terns heading southwards along the east coast of Britain. The autumn migration, when millions of birds leave the British Isles and head south and millions of birds from the north arrive here, largely goes on unseen.

Feeding niches of shore waders

Many people look out over one of our large estuaries or bays, such as the Ribble or Solway, and Morecambe Bay or the Wash, at low water and consider that the vast expanse of shore is quite uniform. Nothing could be further from the truth! Put on a pair of gumboots and walk across it. Some parts are quite sticky ooze, some parts firm mud. The higher banks may be composed of quite golden sand, while the majority of the shore is a silty, sandy mud. The casts of lugworms – probably the only clue of life beneath the surface – are not evenly distributed, for they are more abundant towards the low-water mark but also occur in high densities in the wetter, siltier depressions on the middle shore.

Clearly the shore, between high- and low-water marks, is a mosaic of 'ecological niches' based on the sort of material found there (sand, sandy mud, silt, mud, and so on), how well drained that part of the shore is, and how close that part of the shore is to the low-water mark. Observations of lugworm casts, backed up with a little delving around with a garden trowel, will confirm that the shore invertebrates, on which the immense flocks of waders feed, occur abundantly in some niches but not others.

Visit the same estuary and bay at high water and watch one of the wader roosts at the top of the shore as the tide recedes, and then try to follow one or two of the more numerous species to their low-water feeding areas. Notice that some, like the oystercatcher, may wait for up to two hours before they leave their roost and head off directly to the silty-mud banks of the lower shore to feed on cockles. By way of contrast, watch carefully the knots. They remain tightly packed in their roost for up to an hour after the tide has started to fall and then move straight down to the water's edge. Here they feed keenly, pecking at the surface of the wet mud. What they are feeding on here is a tiny snail called the laver spire-shell that occurs in millions in a muddy niche on the middle-to-upper shore. However, there is very little food value in laver spire-shells, so as soon as the silty-mud banks of the lower shore are exposed, the clouds of knots fly out to them. There, over the period of extreme low water, the knots feed on an orange-pink bivalve mollusc called the Baltic tellin, which occurs in abundance only in that niche.

There may be a flock of sanderlings in the high-water roost in September and October. They have a completely different feeding niche, for they feed almost exclusively on the sandy beaches. But watch them carefully. Mostly they feed at the edge of the tide, following it down the shore on the ebb and back up on the flood. What is surprising is that when the sand on which they have just been feeding has dried out, there is nothing living in it that could be described as food. A few moments with a very fine-meshed net at the water's edge provides the answer, however. Huge numbers of tiny crustaceans follow the tide back and forth over the sandy shore, and it is on these that the sanderlings feed. Hence, their main feeding niche is sandy shores where the sea is lapping.

Some waders do feed in a wide range of shore niches. The grey plover is a good example. Some feed at the waters's edge on sandy shores, like the sanderling. Others seek tiny marine worms in the wetter hollows on sandy shores. Others feed like the knot at the upper shore on laver spire-shells and on Baltic tellins on the lower shore. Some feed on shrimps and worms in the ooziest mud. If there are mussel banks in the estuary or bay, some grey plovers will be found there. If the bay or estuary has an area of rocky shore, many will go there as the tide falls, to seek crabs and other crustaceans.

GREY
PLOVER

SANDERLING

KNOT

A walk across an estuary shore at low water will reveal the feeding niches of many waders, like the grey plover, knot and sanderling. Some will feed only at the tide edge and others in a wide range of niches.

Some ducks in autumn

During late summer the ducks that have bred in the British Isles moult, and for several weeks they seem drab, scruffy affairs. By October, though, the moult is completed and they appear in new spick-and-span plumage. The first of those ducks that have bred elsewhere in northern Europe begin to arrive on British estuaries, marshes and lakes in September. Their numbers rapidly increase in October and November to reach a peak in midwinter. They have already moulted when they arrive, though some of the feathers may not have fully developed. For instance, it is often not until the end of October that the long central tail feathers of the drake pintail complete their growth.

Many species of ducks occur in large numbers in the British Isles from autumn and through the winter: for instance, totals of over 250,000 wigeon, about 100,000 teal and 150,000 mallard, most of which are autumn immigrants, have been recorded by the Wildfowl Trust's 'National Wildfowl Counts'. Other species, though still fairly common and widespread, occur in smaller numbers.

The shoveler is the archetypal dabbling duck, with its huge serrated bill that it uses to strain food items from the surface of mud or water. Because of the drainage of much of Britain's natural freshwater habitats in the 18th, 19th and early 20th centuries, the shoveler greatly decreased in the British Isles as both a breeding and wintering bird. However, the establishment of many wetland reserves and the construction of large reservoirs and gravel pits in the latter half of the 20th century have led to a slow increase in the numbers of this handsome bird.

By complete contrast, the gadwall was traditionally a very rare British bird that has become quite common in recent years because of introductions by man. These began in the 1850s when wing-clipped birds were introduced into Norfolk, and later into the Home Counties, Gloucestershire and the English Midlands, and established localized feral stocks. In the 1960s, gadwall were introduced by the Wildfowl Trust to their headquarters at Slimbridge in Gloucestershire, and later, in the 1970s, to the Trust's reserve at Martin Mere, Lancashire. At both sanctuaries numbers grew rapidly and some birds left to colonize other sites. The numbers of gadwall in Britain have quickly increased, and the birds have become more widespread. Whereas there were only about 500 gadwall in the British Isles in the early 1960s, today the total reaches over 5000 in autumn.

It is also worth noting that another species also owes its presence and increasing numbers on British lakes to man: the North American ruddy duck. This species was first 'accidentally' released by the Wildfowl Trust at Slimbridge in the 1950s and quickly became established on the reservoirs of the Bristol area and north and west Midlands. By the late 1980s, it was reported breeding from a wide variety of lakes throughout England and Wales. Birds arrive on a new water after the breeding season, overwinter and breed there the following year. In this way the increase continues.

A third species that is at home equally on inshore waters and on freshwater lakes is the goldeneye. Though a few pairs do now breed in Britain, they are insignificant compared with the much larger numbers that arrive from Scandinavia in autumn for the winter. Unlike the gadwall and shoveler, which dabble for their food or occasionally up-end in very shallow water, the goldeneye is a diving duck. In the sea it feeds on crabs, shrimps and small mussels, and in lakes it looks for freshwater shrimps, caddis larvae, mayfly nymphs and water boatmen.

Among the commoner ducks that might occur on your local lake it is worth keeping an eye open in autumn and winter for scarcer species like the shoveler, gadwall and goldeneye.

GOLDENEYE

♀

♂

GADWALL

♂

♀

♀

♂

Pheasant coverts

The pheasant is not a native British bird. Some ornithologists have considered that it was introduced by the Romans, others that the Normans brought it across from Europe in the 11th century. Both are perhaps correct, for these invaders of Britain were fond of taking with them, wherever they went, some of their favourite foods from home. By the end of the 19th century pheasants had been introduced to most parts of the British Isles to provide for the increasingly popular sport of shooting.

Pheasants were carefully preserved for sport on most of the major estates. Gamekeepers were employed to reduce the 'vermin' that might threaten the pheasant stocks and to prevent poaching. Special areas of deciduous woodland, usually arranged in long, narrow and sometimes L-shaped strips, were planted as special pheasant coverts. Often an understorey of rhododendrons was also planted. Each day the gamekeeper would scatter grain in the coverts (see also page 30). Thus, these coverts provided the pheasants with shelter and kept them concentrated in one place so that on shooting days the bag would be as big as possible.

Eventually, it was realized that allowing the pheasants to breed naturally was not the ideal way to produce good shooting. It therefore became policy to trap the birds remaining at the end of the shooting season so that the eggs were laid in captivity. These eggs were then incubated under broody hens or in incubators and the young hand-reared. This is still the usual pattern today. Thus, most of the pheasants shot in the British Isles are not really 'wild'.

Interestingly, the pheasant is not really a woodland bird. In its native Asia and south-eastern Russia it is a bird of the fens and freshwater marshes. So perhaps it is not unexpected that some of the thriving feral populations occur on reed-covered peat bogs in Ireland and parts of Scotland.

Many birdwatchers are opposed to the sport of shooting. Certainly in the past the populations of many of our more interesting carnivorous mammals and birds were brought to the verge of extinction in the name of game preservation. However, there is another side to the argument. Over large parts of the countryside the only significant woodlands that have been allowed to remain are pheasant coverts, and without these coverts many woodland birds would have disappeared.

The jay is a typical example. This is more of a woodland species than any of the other crows. The maintenance of broad-leaved pheasant coverts over much of lowland England has helped maintain the widespread distribution of the jay, especially woodlands that contain oak trees, which provide the jay with its favourite autumn food of acorns.

The green woodpecker is another example. Whilst the spotted woodpeckers occur commonly in larger and denser woodlands, the green woodpecker prefers small scattered copses with open spaces between. This is because the green woodpecker obtains much of its food, such as ants and insect larvae, from amongst open turf. Large sporting estates provide such a habitat, with pheasant coverts separated by stretches of pasture and parkland. Throughout much of its range, therefore, the green woodpecker owes its existence to countryside that is manicured for sport with the pheasant.

In so many regions, from the flatlands of East Anglia and the wolds of Lincolnshire and east Yorkshire to the coastal plain of north-west England, pheasant coverts are woodland oases in the midst of the desert of arable farmland. Oases for a variety of woodland birds.

Many areas of woodland are strictly preserved for the pheasant. They are also havens for a wide variety of wild woodland birds, such as the jay and green woodpecker.

GREEN WOODPECKER

JAY

PHEASANT

Bird of the month: Collared dove

No species of bird throughout history has colonized the British Isles like the collared dove. It seems incredible now that, as a young birdwatcher in the mid-1950s, I had never heard of the collared dove. Yet today, 35 years later, they are often ignored because they are so common!

Up to 1930, in order to see a collared dove in Europe one had to travel east, to Turkey, Bulgaria and Albania. Then the species suddenly exploded from its range: an avian *Blitzkrieg*! Hungary was colonized in 1932; they reached Czechoslovakia in 1936 and Austria in 1938. The momentum increased following the colonization of Germany in 1943, for then, in the space of six years to 1952, collared doves swept into the Netherlands, Denmark, Sweden, Switzerland, France, Belgium and Norway. It was three years later, in 1955, that the English Channel and North Sea barrier was crossed and they were first recorded in Britain, on the Norfolk coast. It was in the same year that collared doves first nested in Britain, once again in Norfolk.

The species spread relatively slowly at first in Britain. By 1958 there were isolated pockets – each of them possibly originating from separate invasions from mainland Europe – as far apart as Inverness, Strathclyde, Co. Durham and Kent. From these centres, the increasing population spread and new isolated populations were founded: for example, in Devon and Dublin by 1960. Further consolidation by the breeding stock, supported by reinforcements of foreign immigrants, saw the colonization of West Wales, Cornwall and the Hebrides by 1962. By 1965, the northernmost Shetlands had collared doves. And ten years later, when the BTO published *The Atlas of Breeding Birds in Britain and Ireland*, the only places without a resident population of collared doves were the barren uplands of Scotland, the Pennines and Wales, and the peat boglands of central Ireland.

Collared doves have maintained a very close relationship with man throughout their spread, perhaps exploiting a niche that has never been completely filled by any other species; that of urban and suburban countryside. They are frequently found in large mature gardens, town parks and allotments. At the edges of towns and in villages, they seem particularly fond of small-holdings, especially with free-range poultry runs. On the northern mainland of Scotland and in the islands, they are commonly found in the strip crofts. By contrast, they are infrequently found in expanses of arable country, a habitat where the wood pigeon and closely-related turtle dove are dominant. One often finds, for instance, turtle doves and wood pigeons feeding in the midst of huge modern barley and wheat fields in East Anglia and the Lincolnshire and Yorkshire Wolds; but rarely a collared dove. In the villages and around the farmsteads of these regions, however, the collared dove is the dominant species.

During the 1960s, the collared dove population of the British Isles increased by a phenomenal 100 per cent per annum. But as suitable habitat became colonized, the rate of increase slowed down until, by the late 1980s, the population stabilized.

Why did such a relatively sedentary species suddenly change its habits and increase in numbers and extend its range so suddenly and so rapidly? Perhaps it was a response to a change in our human ecology, which had produced a suitable niche through Europe in earlier times. Perhaps a genetic mutation, which enabled a higher reproduction output and some sort of migratory urge, occurred and then spread through the original collared dove population. No one knows for sure.

All birdwatchers know the collared dove. But it has been a British bird only since 1955.

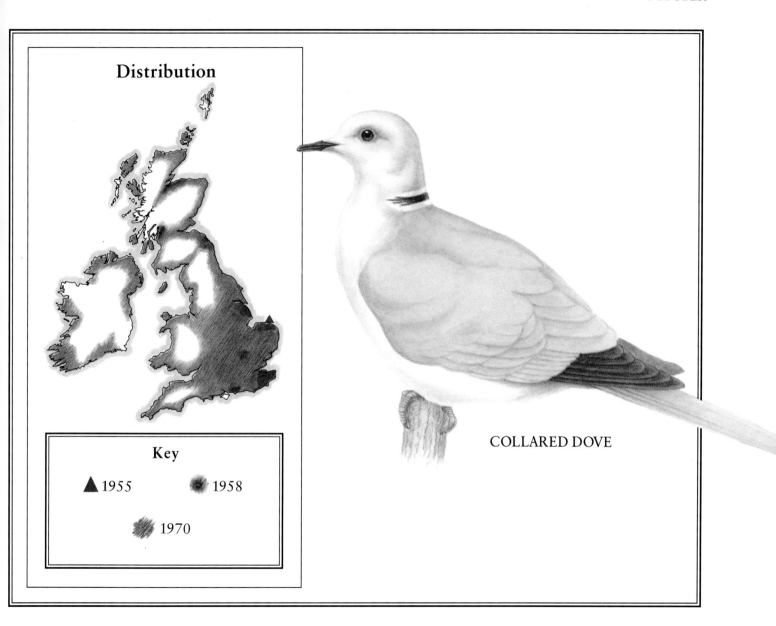

Distribution

Key

▲ 1955   1958

     1970

COLLARED DOVE

Vagrancy

One of the great joys of birdwatching is watching the unusual; of finding and identifying a rare bird. This thrill is all the greater when the bird is one that is unexpected – one that ought not to be there. A bird that really should be thousands of miles away. Such extremely rare birds are known as vagrants, and the best chance of watching a vagrant comes in autumn when millions of birds are travelling throughout the world from summer quarters to winter quarters. Always a few, especially young birds, take the wrong bearing and end up in the British Isles.

Vagrants have possibly four different origins, at least two of which are predictable and give the best chance of seeing one. Each autumn, numbers of birds leave Canada and the northern states of the USA and head south to winter in South America. Numbers – possibly several hundreds of them – may become disorientated and then be blown by prevailing westerly winds towards Europe. Species like the buff-breasted sandpiper, pectoral sandpiper and semi-palmated sandpiper might then occur on sewage farms or muddy coastal pools. Ring-billed and Bonaparte's gulls may be found feeding with our British gulls on the local rubbish tip or around a fish dock. A hermit thrush, red-eyed vireo or blackpoll warbler may be discovered flitting in undergrowth. The array of American species that might be found in the British Isles is huge: go to the Scilly Isles in October and you are sure to see several.

The second class of vagrants are those of eastern origin, from Siberia and eastern Europe. Given a strong easterly airstream over those regions, lots of commoner migrants (such as lesser whitethroats, willow warblers and fieldfares) will arrive on the east coast. Among them will be scarce but quite regular migrants like the great grey shrike and wryneck, and perhaps one or two vagrants. There may be a Radde's warbler or greenish warbler; perhaps a great snipe. Go to Fair Isle in the Shetlands, one of the most famous places to see vagrants, in October and almost anything may turn up: a yellow-breasted bunting, citrine wagtail, two-barred crossbill, lanceolated warbler, pechora pipit – such rarities are common on Fair Isle!

Many vagrants are sea birds and to find them you have to watch the sea! Sometimes a vagrant may settle down for long periods with one of the colonies of common birds, such as the lesser crested tern that joined the Sandwich terns on the Farnes (it should have been in the Persian Gulf!) or the black-browed albatross from the South Atlantic that lived with the gannets on the Bass Rock, East Lothian. These birds become quite famous and hundreds of birdwatchers travel to see them. A trip to Cape Clear Bird Observatory in Ireland, which overlooks the Western Approaches and the Atlantic, is perhaps as good a place as any to see a vagrant sea bird flying past. Or take one of the specially chartered boat trips from Cornwall that head out into the Western Approaches in search of species like the Antarctic Wilson's petrel.

The really special vagrants are the ones that are completely unpredictable. One might appear at any time and anywhere, though autumn is perhaps the best time. Once, I arrived on the Hebridean island of Islay in October and found, on my way to the cottage, a harlequin duck swimming close inshore. This would have come from Iceland or, more probably, Greenland. In 1977 an Eleonora's falcon, which ought to have been in the Mediterranean region, spent two days hunting Formby Point in Lancashire. In 1968 a spectacled warbler, which normally occurs no nearer to the British Isles than the Mediterranean, arrived at Spurn Head in Humberside.

Right A Harlequin duck, blown off course to the west coast of Scotland. In autumn many migrating birds lose their way. Every year several of these vagrants, from North America, eastern Europe, the Arctic and Asia find themselves in the British Isles and are eagerly sought by birdwatchers.

Rushy bogs

One habitat that has declined greatly during the 20th century is wet, rushy grassland, dissected by weedy ditches. All too often, farmers have considered such areas as 'unproductive'; they have been drained and the ditches filled in. This is a pity for boggy habitats attract a quite special community of birds, both in the breeding season and in winter.

One that I used to study was typical: an area almost a mile in length and half a mile in width, which dried out only in the severest of summer droughts. In winter, the place was alive with water rails, moorhens, mallard, teal and a great variety of waders. Quite rare species, like the spotted crake and bittern, turned up regularly. As many as 112 herons could be watched from the adjacent embankments as they fished for small roach and bream in the shallow dykes. And the place was alive with snipe and jack snipe. In the late afternoon, when the wildfowlers who rented and maintained this bog arrived for the evening flight, hundreds of snipe would take wing and circle to land at a safe distance behind them. One afternoon in late October, I estimated that over 2000 snipe were feeding on this one bog. The numbers of jack snipe were more difficult to assess because they are smaller than the common species, and when disturbed they never fly off calling loudly but instead fly low and silently for a few yards before landing. However, one November day, by carefully walking across the bog with some friends, all in line, we came up with a total of 47 jack snipe for the area.

Then, one dry summer the farmer brought heavy machinery to the bog. Tile drains were laid across it in a herring-bone arrangement. The shallow dykes were deepened and their weedy margins made sterile with steep, high, bare clay banks. In September, the area was ploughed and more cereal crops raised for the EEC stockpile. The snipe, jack snipe, herons and wildfowl did not return that autumn.

By contrast, in 1975 that great conservationist and wildfowl expert the late Jeffery Harrison took me to a bog at the edge of the Sevenoaks Gravel Pit Reserve in Kent, where there was formerly hardly any bog. Following negotiations with the farmer, a tiny stream had been dammed to flood 0.8 acres and raise the water table over an area of three acres. The effect was incredible, for the managed bog then began to attract large numbers of snipe and jack snipe. Why cannot local natural history societies throughout the British Isles do the same?

It is interesting to note that so many of the birds that occur on freshwater bogs and marshes tend to be fairly inactive during the day and feed between dusk and dawn. And that many species, especially the snipe, jack snipe and heron, will leave their daytime refuges to seek out new feeding areas. At dusk, even in built-up areas, the 'snape' notes of the common snipe may be heard overhead and the big silhouette and 'kraak' cry of the heron noted in the half-light. During one night, they may visit several sites in search of food. A piece of floodwater may hold no fish for the heron, so it will move on. Yet the wet margins may provide soft-enough soil and a sufficiently high earthworm population for the snipe and jack snipe to feed through until dawn.

The wet, rushy field next to my home is a case in point. At present, only one blackbird and four meadow pipits are feeding there now. This evening, scores of snipe and one or two jack snipe will visit, together with three herons that fish the ditches. Tomorrow morning, the only trace of them will be the probe marks of the snipe and perhaps the fishy droppings and large footprints of the herons. But next year there are plans to develop this field!

Each year more wetlands are drained. And as one area is lost, so too is another feeding ground for wetland birds such as the snipe, jack snipe and heron.

JACK SNIPE

GREY HERON

SNIPE

Winter visitors

Through the autumn and continuing well into November, huge numbers of winter visitors arrive in the British Isles. These include flocks of waders and wildfowl, gulls, sea birds such as the little auk, and several species of land birds.

Two species of thrushes are the most conspicuous of land birds that stream into the country: the fieldfare and redwing. All our winter fieldfares originate from the extensive birch and pine forests of Scandinavia and the Soviet Union. Large birds, almost as big as our resident mistle thrushes, they migrate across the North Sea and then roam the countryside in large flocks. They are quite easy to identify, not only by their plumage but also by the loud 'chacking' call that they make as they fly overhead or jostle in bushes for food.

Redwings have two completely different origins. Some come, like the fieldfares, from north-eastern Europe. Others come from Iceland. Redwings are smaller than fieldfares, being about the size of our native song thrushes. They, too, generally occur in flocks. They are also easy to identify at close quarters by their distinct eye-stripe, and in flight by the dark red patch under their wings. Their call note is also very distinctive: a thin 'seeep'. It is also possible, when you get to know redwings really well, to identify the origins of a flock, for the Icelandic birds are darker than the Scandinavian birds.

Redwings and fieldfares are particularly fond of berries. At many east-coast sites, where the birds make their first landfalls after their long journey across the sea, they throng into clumps of sea buckthorn and replenish their energy reserves on the orange berries. Then, as they spread inland, they seek the red haws of hawthorn hedges, the berries of the rowan and rose hips, and even the last of the brambles and elderberries. Several hundreds may arrive one morning and completely strip a bush or hedgerow before moving on.

It is noticeable that redwings and fieldfares appear to be more abundant in the late autumn than in the middle of winter, and that numbers seem to increase in late winter from late February through March. This is because a large number of birds that arrive here in autumn continue their migration southwards, into mainland Europe, and later stop off again on their return spring migration.

Although redwings and fieldfares are the most conspicuous of land birds to visit us in winter, many other species do the same. The numbers of our resident robins and blackbirds are joined by large numbers from Scandinavia, while some of the starlings that squabble on our bird-tables may have come from as far away as Moscow.

One bird that is worth looking for, especially in late autumn, is the firecrest. With the goldcrest, this is the smallest of British birds. Of course, the goldcrest is quite a common breeding bird, especially in mixed or open coniferous woodlands, but only a few pairs of firecrests breed in Britain, most of them in southern England. So the best chance of seeing one is on the coast (especially the east coast) in October or early November, when it has just completed its migration.

Firecrests are not easy to spot, however. First get to know the commoner goldcrest well and it is then much easier. The firecrest has a much more solid, low-pitched 'zit' call, compared with the fragile, shrill 'zeee-zeeee-zeeec' note of the goldcrest. Then, when you see the bird, there can be no doubt: with its conspicuous white superciliary eye-stripe that is bordered with black stripes, its almost white underparts and brighter green upperparts, there is no mistaking the firecrest.

REDWING

FIRECREST

No one should find it difficult to watch redwings and fieldfares, for they are very common winter visitors to the British Isles. By contrast, it takes a lot of effort and some luck to find a firecrest.

FIELDFARE

Spectacular wildfowl

Wildfowl should not be seen singly, especially in winter. They should always be seen in flocks, and the bigger the flock the better. Wildfowl are also seen at their best in wild habitats and, though some might argue that this is a personal preference, without the comfort of a hide. Certainly, the sight of large herds of swans and flocks of ducks and geese from the large hides at Martin Mere (Lancashire), Welney (Cambridgeshire), and Slimbridge (Gloucestershire) is splendid, and offers a superb chance of watching the birds at close quarters and of learning how to identify them. But it is not to be compared with watching them out in open country.

To sit, just before dawn, on an estuary embankment by Morecambe Bay, the Ribble or Solway and hear, far out on the wet mudflats, the grumblings of several thousand roosting pink-footed geese is thrilling. Then, as the light slowly breaks in the eastern sky, their grumblings increase to a crescendo as they rise from their roost and head across the shore. Suddenly they are there, low overhead, all of them calling loudly 'pink-wink... pink-wink'. A mass of blurred grey splodges arranged in long strings and loose V-formations within a tight pack. To be in the same place in the late afternoon and watch skein after skein flighting out from their inland feeding areas and on to the tideway for the night is no less spectacular.

A similarly exciting experience is watching big flocks of ducks flighting over an estuary on the tide. During the past 25 years, the Mersey and Dee estuaries have become one of the major European wintering grounds of the pintail, with flocks totalling 20,000. During the low-water period, the pintail scatter across the oozy mudflats, feeding on tiny invertebrates. But as the tide pushes them off the mud they flight on to the salt-marshes that border the estuary, either to feed on seeds and fruits of the marsh plants or simply to rest. As you sit and watch, from the windswept embankment, wave after wave of pintail, together with teal, mallard and wigeon, settle on the flooding marsh. In fact, so dense can the birds become that through a telescope the marsh looks distinctly chocolate-brown, because of the concentration of drake pintail heads sticking up from the long vegetation.

Strangely enough, few birdwatchers ever go birdwatching at night, believing that there is little to see. This is not true, though, for some birds are most active at night. Wigeon often spend the daylight hours sleeping on the tide, frequently out of view. But then, when it is dark, they flight on to the grassy salt-marshes to feed under the light of the moon. Sit on the marsh embankment and watch and listen. Save for the grumbling of the pink-feet in their roost, and the piping of an occasional oystercatcher, there is nothing but silence. Then, as the moon begins to rise, a clamour of explosive shrill calls anounces that the wigeon are on the move. 'Wheeeoo', they call. 'Wheeooo .. wheeeooo'. Thousands of black shapes pass, in dense clouds, through the inky night sky. Some are briefly silhouetted against the moon as they turn into the wind before landing. Then everything goes quiet. But on a still night, when the birds are feeding high on the marsh, the rasping sounds made by thousands of bills tearing at the sweet fescue grass are clearly audible.

Remember, do not neglect the reserves where wildfowl can be watched from hides at close quarters. Do not neglect to watch the small parties of wildfowl that appear on small pools and flooded meadows. But similarly, do not neglect the opportunities we have in the British Isles for watching large flocks of wild geese and ducks in wild places.

One of the greatest ornithological spectacles is huge flocks of wildfowl: thousands of wigeon, pintail, pink-feet and other species of ducks and geese flighting over an estuary or fen.

PINTAIL

PINK-FOOTED GOOSE

WIGEON

Bird of the month: Little auk

The little auk (or dovekie) is a species that most people never come across in the British Isles, but is one which can easily be watched provided that the right places are visited at the right time of the year.

The breeding range of the little auk is the high Arctic. The nearest and perhaps most southerly colony is on the island of Grimsey, off the north coast of Iceland, which is just north of the Arctic Circle. Further north, it nests on Spitzbergen, Bear Island, Jan Mayen, and on the Soviet archipelagos of Novaya Zemlya and Franz Josef Land. Immense numbers, totalling several millions, breed on the cliffs around the coast of Greenland.

Then, with the build-up of the pack ice in autumn, the little auks are pushed southwards towards the Atlantic. Many concentrate at the edge of the ice where they feed on tiny planktonic crustaceans. But large numbers also move along the Norwegian coast and into the North Sea, and into the Atlantic, especially on the western side, off Newfoundland.

Generally, little auks do not come close to land out of their nesting season, especially those birds that overwinter in the North Sea and north-east Atlantic. But the fact that they are out there, somewhere, can be gauged from observations made from ships and oil platforms where little auks are regularly seen. However, given the right weather conditions, it is easy to watch this diminutive sea bird; and November is possibly the best month in which to do so.

What is needed is a gale-force wind blowing from the direction of north-north-west to north-east. At several sites, especially on the north coast of Scotland and north-east coast of England, little auks will be blown close inshore. At places like Fife Ness in Scotland, Emanuel Head on Lindisfarne, and Flamborough and Spurn Heads in Humberside, small parties may be seen flying with fast wingbeats low over the waves – tiny black-and-white specks amidst the white surf of the raging sea. Small numbers may also fly past much closer, often along the tide edge. Occasionally, at Spurn and Fife Ness in particular, little auks that have been blown into the Humber or Forth may fly overland to regain the open sea. And, most incredibly, a flock of starlings might fly to join them. A case of mistaken identity on the part of the starlings, for the two quite different species bear some resemblance to each other in flight (save for the white underparts of the little auk).

During periods of severe gales, a 'wreck' of little auks may occur. Then, large numbers of birds, sometimes totalling thousands, are blown inshore and can be seen in bays, estuaries and harbours, and on holiday-town boating lakes. Many may be blown far inland and found exhausted, lying in fields, on roads, or even in town centres. Few parts of the British Isles have no record of little auks, wrecked during a violent November storm.

It ought to be mentioned that similar conditions – severe gales, but in this case of a more westerly direction – often provide excellent opportunities for watching another sea bird that is scarce in the British Isles. The Leach's petrel migrates southwards through the Atlantic in November. Usually it keeps well offshore, but from a suitable west-coast vantage point – such as Formby Point in Lancashire and South Walney in Cumbria – small numbers, perhaps totalling ten or more individuals, are recorded each year under the correct weather conditions. Again, should the gale reach storm force then wrecks of Leach's petrels may occur, with birds blown far inland. Following one such wreck, in November 1963, I even found a Leach's petrel crouching in the corner of a bus shelter in the middle of Preston late at night!

The diminutive little auk usually winters close to the arctic pack ice or on the sea far from land. But small parties can be readily seen through the winter provided you go to the right place in the right weather conditions.

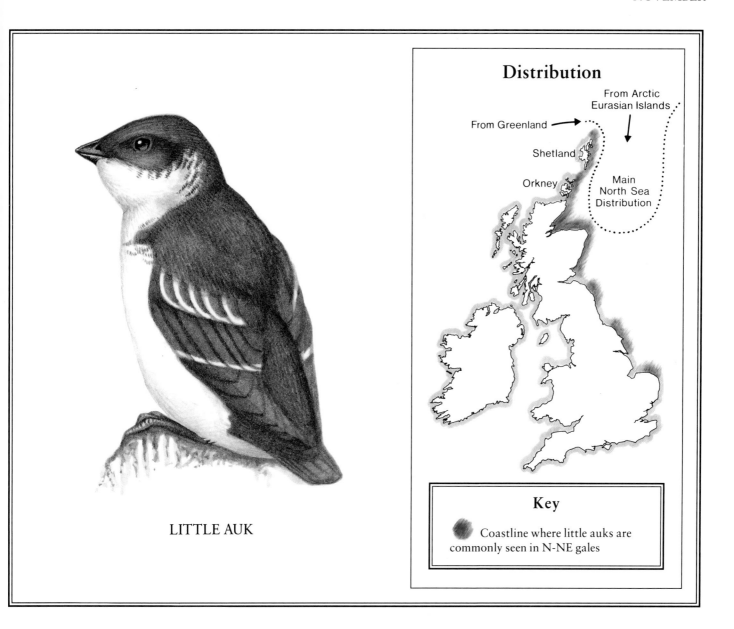

LITTLE AUK

Distribution

From Arctic
Eurasian Islands

From Greenland →

Shetland

Orkney

Main
North Sea
Distribution

Key

Coastline where little auks are commonly seen in N-NE gales

Daily routine in winter

Most birds are strictly diurnal: they are active through the hours of daylight. In the late winter afternoon, pigeons, thrushes, crows, starlings and finches collect together in large flocks and then, as night falls, settle in trees or bushes to roost. Throughout the late afternoon, long strings of gulls can be watched almost anywhere in the British Isles as they fly to their roosts on reservoirs or estuaries. Then at dawn the roosts break up quickly as the birds scatter across the surrounding countryside in search of food.

Some birds, though, are nocturnal in their daily routine. Through the hours of daylight they roost, and at sunset they awaken and fly off in search of food. Owls are perhaps the most famous of nocturnal birds, though only the long-eared, tawny and little owls are truly nocturnal. The short-eared owl, which haunts inland bogs and coastal marshes in winter, will feed throughout the day, and the barn owl is often seen hunting in broad daylight in winter. Some of the duck species are also nocturnal in their winter routine. For example, mallard and teal will often spend the day sleeping and loafing amongst reedbeds; at nightfall, they head off to arable farmland to feed through the night.

Wild geese, such as the pink-foot and white-front, show both diurnal and nocturnal behaviour. Each day they leave their roosting grounds, usually on estuary mudflats, for the stubbles, potato fields and meadows inland. Then at dusk they flight back to the shore to roost. However, on nights around full moon the geese will leave their roost as the moon rises and head inland to feed, returning to the shore should the moon set before dawn.

Some birds are said to be crepuscular in their daily routine, because they have their main feeding periods in the half-light of dusk and dawn. Just before dusk, it is quite common to see herons flighting from their daylight roosts to feed in shallow pools, rivers and estuaries; and then to hear them calling overhead a couple of hours later as they fly back to roost. In the reed fenlands, bitterns are far more active around dusk and dawn; these are by far the best times to see them as they spend the day hidden in the dense reeds.

The daily routine of some shore birds, such as the oystercatcher, curlew, turnstone, redshank, dunlin and knot, is controlled primarily by the tide cycle, though the daily cycle also plays a part. At high water, these waders are forced from their mudflat feeding grounds. Many retire to the top of the shore and sleep in tightly-packed roosts until the tide ebbs. However, some oystercatchers, curlews and redshanks may leave the shore altogether and join with lapwings and golden plovers to feed on wet coastal pastures. A proportion of these may stay feeding on the farmlands until dusk, when they return to the shore to feed through the night. Others, however, will leave the fields as the tide ebbs and arrive on their mudflat feeding grounds just as the ebbing tide exposes them. How these birds manage to time this flight perfectly is quite incredible. The timing of high water changes each day by roughly an hour, and the height that the tide flows up and ebbs down the shore varies widely through a lunar tidal cycle. Yet they can predict quite accurately when to leave the farmland, often several miles inland, and arrive on their patch of mudflat at precisely the right time.

In winter the period of daylight is very short. Those birds, such as birds of prey, gulls and passerines, which need to see clearly when feeding, have no choice: they are forced to stop feeding at dusk. However, those that have good night vision, such as waders and wildfowl, have developed daily routines to take advantage of any opportunity to collect food.

Right A short-eared owl, hunting during a late winter afternoon, takes a starling from a flock returning to roost. Winter routines are fascinating to watch; among the most spectacular are the dawn and dusk and full-moon flights of wild geese as they pass between estuary roost and farmland feeding areas.

Woodland birds and a question of size

Many people look at the picture in a bird book but fail to notice the statistic given in the verbal description: length. The result is that although they know the bird's plumage, they cannot identify the bird because they don't know how big it is! And with so many birds, the illustrations of plumage *suggest* that the bird is bigger than it really is! The kingfisher is a good example. Often I have taken people who have never seen a kingfisher to a river where kingfishers abound. When eventually a kingfisher is clearly seen for the first time, the comment is usually: 'They are so tiny. I expected them to be so big.' (The hands are then separated by a foot or more.)

Many birdwatchers fall into the same trap with certain woodland birds. Nuthatches are thought to be as big as thrushes, rather than slightly smaller than the house sparrow. Treecreepers are imagined to be starling size; certainly not smaller than the great tit! Even more ludicrous, woodpeckers are commonly thought of as crow size by birdwatchers who have never seen one but keep trying to do so.

Some statistics are required. One textbook gives the following lengths, from tip of bill to end of tail:

blue tit – $4\frac{1}{2}$ in.
house sparrow – $5\frac{3}{4}$ in.
starling – $8\frac{1}{2}$ in.
song thrush – 8 in.
blackbird – 10 in.
carrion crow – $18\frac{1}{2}$ in.

The same book gives the length of the great spotted woodpecker as 9 in. and the lesser spotted woodpecker as $5\frac{3}{4}$ in. So when we go out to look for these woodpeckers, we are looking for birds that are the size of the song thrush and the house sparrow respectively. To put this in perspective 'in the field', it is worth cutting two crude woodpecker outlines, from a piece of cardboard, 9 in. and $5\frac{3}{4}$ in. long and colouring them appropriately with felt-tip pens. Then pin them on tree branches in the wood and look at them through binoculars from 20 or 30 yards away. *That* is the size of the woodpeckers you have been searching for.

Once you have the idea of size and scale, then start looking for the real birds. However, cardboard cutouts will not fly away. They are easy to watch! The real woodpeckers can be quite shy and secretive. That is why the best time to watch them is in winter when the tree branches are bare.

Lesser spotted woodpeckers tend to occur in the higher branches of the trees and are best located by their characteristic call: a shrill 'pee-pee-pee-pee'. The little bird can then be located with binoculars. By contrast, great spotted woodpeckers are more silent, though sometimes they can be located by their 'chick-chick' call. Usually they are first seen in flight after they have been disturbed. Like all woodpeckers, they are easy to identify in the air by their distinctly undulating flight. And provided a slow, careful approach is made, the bird can then be tracked down as it feeds on the tree trunks and branches.

How big is a sparrowhawk? They *must* be fairly big, for they feed on small- and medium-sized woodland birds! Male sparrowhawks are in fact little bigger than a blackbird, and the females are about as big as a woodpigeon – and this includes their proportionally very long tails. I have known sparrowhawks that have been gliding through trees to be mistaken for mistle thrushes and collared doves, because they were 'too small' to be sparrowhawks!

Remember when you are learning to identify a species of bird, do not just look at the pictures in the textbooks. Be sure to read the descriptions and make a special note about size.

Some of our most beautiful woodland birds, such as the great and lesser spotted woodpeckers and sparrowhawk, are much smaller than many people imagine.

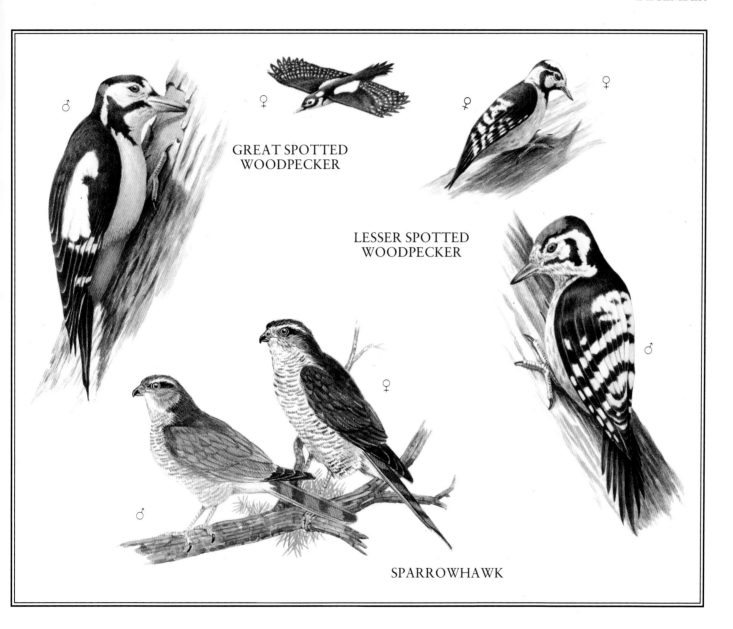

GREAT SPOTTED
WOODPECKER

LESSER SPOTTED
WOODPECKER

SPARROWHAWK

Birds of the winter moors

British moorlands are alive with birds in spring and summer; but in winter, birds are most conspicuous by their absence over much of these uplands. Gone are the meadow pipits and skylarks, the most abundant nesters on the moor. Like the lapwings, curlews, golden plovers and dunlins, these are either on lowland coastal habitats or further south on the European mainland. It is a problem of food. Most of the summer visitors to the uplands feed on insects, and at higher altitudes there are no insects available. They are hidden deep in the peat and often protected by frost, ice and snow. What few birds do remain on the open moors are either vegetarians, feeding on the seeds, fruits and shoots of moorland plants, or meat-eaters, feeding on sheep carrion or lesser birds, blue hares or voles.

At the moorland edge, where there is a mosaic of woodland, scrubby grassland and open moor, there may be a population of black grouse. This is a species that has declined greatly during the last 100 years. Today it is found mostly in Wales, south Cumbria and the northern Pennines, the Scottish Borders north to the Central Lowlands, and through much of the forested uplands of northern Scotland. Once it was widespread through much of the English Midlands, East Anglia and the south-west, but now only tiny numbers remain in Staffordshire and Devon.

In early winter on the Northumbrian hills, the black grouse concentrate on the berries of rowan and hawthorn at the moorland edge. Occasionally they move down into the valleys in search of berries and barley stubbles. When the berry crop is exhausted, they then turn to eating tree buds, sedge fruits and grass seeds.

It is very easy to overlook black grouse, even where they are common. More than one birdwatcher has dismissed a party of black cocks (the males) that are feeding in a rushy bog as moorhens! Solitary grey hens that are perched in hawthorns are very easy to overlook, for they are well camouflaged and fly away quietly as one approaches. The black grouse, for many people, is one of those birds where seeing the first is very difficult and takes much time, but after that they seem easy to find!

Over much of the uplands of the British Isles, one or two species of the crow family are almost certain to be seen in winter. In Ireland, the Isle of Man and north-west Scotland this might be the hooded crow and in the rest of Scotland, England and Wales the carrion crow; these also occur in the lowlands. However, another species, the raven, lives predominantly on the mountains and moorlands. These species will be seen as they fly over the moor in search of food, primarily carrion.

Some birdwatchers have difficulty separating the raven and carrion crow. The larger size and heavier build of the raven is really only noticeable when the two are seen together. However, the pointed, diamond-shaped tail of the raven and rounded tail of the carrion crow are diagnostic. So, too, are their calls: a deeply resonant 'crunk-crunk' in the raven and a less resonant 'crahw' in the carrion crow.

There is one very special winter visitor – the snow bunting. Most birdwatchers associate the snow bunting with the sea shore, for in winter small parties can sometimes be seen rooting through the strand line for seeds. However, large flocks, numbering 100 or more, can often be found feeding on the high sedge moors. When they are on the ground feeding, snow buntings are very difficult to see for they blend in so well with the browns and greys of the moor. But as they take flight, their white wing patches and twittering call make them most conspicuous.

SNOW
BUNTING

RAVEN

♂

BLACK GROUSE

♀

Though the moors of northern Britain are almost birdless in winter, the birds that do occur – the black grouse, raven and snow bunting, for example – make a crisp, frosty winter walk over the tops very rewarding.

Winter on the mussel scaups

Edible mussels can only occur on the lower shore where there is a solid foundation to which they can attach themselves. This may be rock or stable, concreted areas of shingle. The mussels themselves provide food for birds that have the ability to obtain the flesh from between the two thick, hard shells. The oystercatcher (see page 92) commonly feeds on mussels, which it can open in one of two ways. Some oystercatchers obtain the mussel meat by smashing open the shells with powerful blows from their sturdy bills. Others are more subtle in their approach: they are 'stabbers'. They creep up on the mussels that still have their shells open in shallow water. And then, with a quick stab, they sever the 'adductor muscle', which the mussel uses to close the shells, thus preventing the mussel from shutting. They can then take their time in winkling out the meat.

Some birds devour the mussels whole. Tiny mussels, known as 'spat', are often taken by purple sandpipers and turnstones at low water when the mussel scaups are exposed. Eiders, on the other hand, feed over the scaups at high water and dive to gather small- or medium-sized mussels. Some gulls also will devour the smaller mussels whole, shell and all, while others collect larger specimens from the scaups and then fly into the air to drop them from a great height, smashing them. Often gulls will discover particularly hard areas on which to drop these larger mussels to greater effect. One herring gull learned that the corrugated-iron roof of a factory close to the shore was ideal for this purpose

Besides mussels, the scaups also have food in the form of large and diverse populations of other lesser invertebrates: small shrimps, marine worms, periwinkles, shore crabs and, in the pools, small fish.

Purple sandpipers peck and probe in the nooks and crannies for tiny periwinkles and the smaller crustaceans. They are quite special birds in their distribution in the British Isles, for they occur only where the scaups are rocky, and are rarely found on shingle mussel scaups. By contrast, the turnstone occurs on both rocky and shingle shores where it can be seen probing into cavities for food, as well as living up to its name as a 'turn-stone', flicking pebbles over and grabbing any small invertebrate thus disturbed.

As the tide flows, the oystercatchers, purple sandpipers and turnstones retreat to higher ground. As soon as the lower mussels are covered, the oystercatchers usually stop feeding and flight directly to the upper shore where they sleep until the ebb. However, turnstones and purple sandpipers continue feeding in front of the advancing waves, often leaving one boulder or patch of mussels just before a breaking wave washes them away.

As the tide flows, the eiders drift inshore over the mussel banks and begin feeding. Sometimes they will surface with a mussel, sometimes with a large crab. These are swallowed whole, for the tough gizzard of the eider is easily capable of crushing these hard creatures. The crops of the eiders, which store the food before it is digested, are quickly filled and the birds then swim on the high tide to the shore to sleep and digest their meal. On the ebb they drift out once more across the mussel scaups to refill their crops.

Mussel scaups are a fascinating winter habitat for the birdwatcher. They are highly productive habitats, generating huge amounts of food quickly. In some sheltered bays and estuaries, the millions of empty mussel and periwinkle shells (eaten by birds) have accumulated to produce new banks on the shore, which have later been colonized by mussels to produce new scaups. As the scaups have grown, so have the populations of the birds feeding on them.

PURPLE SANDPIPER

TURNSTONE

♀

♂

EIDER

Mussel beds (or scaups) sustain a great diversity of invertebrate life that attracts some quite specialized shore birds, including the eider, turnstone and purple sandpiper.

Birds of the month: Whooper & Bewick's swans

Wild winter swans are exciting to watch because they are huge birds, beautifully majestic and wild! By contrast, our resident mute swans are quite tame and, for many, uninspiring. The wildness of the winter swans is enhanced by their loud musical calls that echo across the expanses of the estuary salt-marshes, freshwater fens and mountain lakes. One can quite imagine, over 1000 years ago, Norse settlers in what we now know as the Lake District watching a newly-arrived herd of whoopers bugling in the midst of Elterwater saying: 'Winter is here!' (Elterwater is the Norse for 'lake of swans'.)

Many birdwatchers find whooper and Bewick's swans very difficult to tell apart. It is really quite easy. Whooper swans are large, almost as big as the mute swan; Bewick's swans are little bigger than farmyard geese. The adults of both species have a yellow patch on their bills, unlike the mute swan, which has a predominantly orange-and-black bill. In the whooper the yellow patch is large and triangular, whereas in the Bewick's swan the patch at the base of the bill is small and rounded. Young whoopers and Bewick's swans are perhaps best identified by size. However, because swan families remain united throughout the winter, it is more convenient to identify the adults and assume that the similarly-sized young swans feeding with them are their offspring from the previous Arctic nesting season.

The majority of the whooper swans that winter in the British Isles breed in Iceland, whereas the Bewick's swans nest in the Arctic Siberian tundra. After the breeding season has ended, the birds moult and then begin to fatten themselves up prior to their

Whooper and Bewick's swans are certainly the most beautiful and romantic of our winter visitors.

BEWICK'S SWAN

WHOOPER SWAN

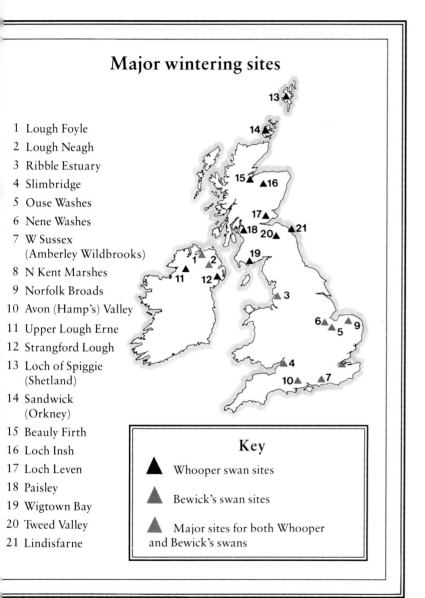

Major wintering sites

1 Lough Foyle

2 Lough Neagh

3 Ribble Estuary

4 Slimbridge

5 Ouse Washes

6 Nene Washes

7 W Sussex
(Amberley Wildbrooks)

8 N Kent Marshes

9 Norfolk Broads

10 Avon (Hamp's) Valley

11 Upper Lough Erne

12 Strangford Lough

13 Loch of Spiggie
(Shetland)

14 Sandwick
(Orkney)

15 Beauly Firth

16 Loch Insh

17 Loch Leven

18 Paisley

19 Wigtown Bay

20 Tweed Valley

21 Lindisfarne

Key

▲ Whooper swan sites

▲ Bewick's swan sites

▲ Major sites for both Whooper
and Bewick's swans

southwards migration. The whooper swans fly to the British Isles direct, a journey of about 500 miles; though from observations in the northern and western isles, some make their first landfalls there before continuing to their main winter refuges. The Bewick's swans' journey is much longer – at least 2000 miles – and they break their migration in the Baltic or on Jutland to rest and refuel. So here in the British Isles we find the first wild swans returning in September or early October. Then, during March and April, the big concentrations at the main swan refuges break up as the birds begin the return to their nesting grounds.

The 20th century has seen a great change in the distribution of wild swans. Formerly, the whooper swan was considered a bird of northern Britain whilst the Bewick's swan was the wild swan of southern Britain. Between 1960 and 1989, numbers began to concentrate at certain places while more ancient swan sites were abandoned or used for just a few days during autumn or spring migration. And areas that had formerly held few wild swans have since become major wintering areas.

The Ribble estuary in Lancashire, which I have been studying since 1960, is a good example. In the early 1960s, both whooper and Bewick's swans were scarce visitors during the migration periods. Then, in the early 1970s, small but increasing numbers began to overwinter. At the same time, the Wildfowl Trust established a reserve at Martin Mere, in Lancashire, where food was put out to attract wild swans. Quickly the populations increased so that, by the late 1980s, up to 600 Bewick's and 400 whoopers were using the Ribble estuary and Martin Mere as their winter quarters. Similarly, on the Ouse Washes in East Anglia: in the 1950s, maxima of 25 whoopers and 620 Bewick's were recorded. But following the establishment of reserves by the RSPB and Wildfowl Trust on the flooded Washes, numbers have grown to over 6000 Bewick's and 600 whoopers.

Winter roosts

In the short days of winter, one of the most fascinating of birdwatching experiences is witnessing the arrival and departure of birds at their roosts. Most birds roost communally, some of them in spectacularly huge numbers. So with a little detective work it is not too difficult tracing them. For us in the British Isles, species like starlings and rooks are probably the easiest to watch roosting because they are such abundant birds and so conspicuous when they gather in their roosts. As early as mid-afternoon, when there is still over an hour of full light remaining, they cease feeding and set off in flocks towards the roost. By locating two or three such flocks in different places, noting carefully the direction of their flight and plotting these flight lines on an Ordnance Survey map, the approximate location of the roost will be discovered where the two or three plotted flight lines intersect. It is then a matter of visiting that place to find the exact location of the roost.

An evening spent watching starlings or rooks gathering at their roost can be quite exciting, particularly if the roost is a big one. They usually do not fly straight into the roost – usually in reedbeds or dense woodland – but carry out a series of mass aerial acrobatics in very close, tight formation above and around the roost site. Perhaps these aerial mass displays are meant to advertise the location of the roost for flocks of birds that have just arrived in the area and are looking for a suitable place to roost. For during the last hour of daylight, more and more lesser flocks may join the ever-increasing congregation as it weaves to and fro in the air.

The roosts of starlings and other small birds are particularly interesting to watch because they attract predators seeking a last meal of the day. Merlins, kestrels, peregrines and sparrowhawks often pursue the roosting birds. In one reedbed, hen harriers and short-eared owls frequently dined on starlings in the late evening. And after nightfall, tawny, little and long-eared owls have been known to take the sleeping birds, judging from the examination of owls' pellets collected close to the roosts.

Mapping the flight lines of birds to and from their roost reveals just how far the members are prepared to go foraging for food during the day. Gulls are particularly interesting, for they are very easy to observe feeding inland on wet pastures and rubbish tips and later flighting in long straggling lines to roost. Often their roosts will be on inland lakes; but sometimes they use these lakes as a gathering place in the afternoon from where they depart in large flocks to the coast. One such roost, on the Ribble estuary in Lancashire, drew gulls from up to 50 miles away.

Wild geese are also easy to track between feeding and roosting grounds. The majority of roosting areas of wild geese are well known and often published either in county *Bird Reports* or in regional bird books. Visit the roost before dawn and watch the directions that the skeins take as they leave the roost. Then spend the day tracing the feeding gaggles. As evening falls, the geese will stop feeding and head for their roost. Whether the birds you have been watching are going to that particular roost can be gauged by taking the bearing of their evening flight line.

Some birds are less conspicuous as they go to roost, but that increases the challenge of studying them. Thrushes often produce loud contact calls as they fly overhead at dusk towards their roost in rhododendron thickets or the yews of a churchyard. Robins and wrens will often utter a snatch of winter song from the bush or ivy-clad tree in which they will spend the night. Watching, investigating and studying birds fully makes our hobby so interesting.

Right *A tawny owl leaves its daytime roost at moonrise. Most birds roost at night, and in winter even the city office worker can look out of the window and watch clouds of starlings circling overhead at dusk, and then see them settling down for the night on window ledges and monuments.*

Bibliography

Bannerman, David (1953 *et seq.*) *The Birds of the British Isles*

B.O.U. (1971) *The Status of Birds in Britain and Ireland*

Campbell, B. and Ferguson-Lees, I. J. (1972) *A Field Guide to Birds' Nests*

Cramp, S. and Simmons, K. E. L. (1977 *et seq.*) *The Birds of the Western Parearctic*

Fuller, R. J. (1982) *Bird Habitats in Britain*

Hollom, P. A. D. (1962) *The Popular Handbook of British Birds* (3rd edn.)

Hollom, P. A. D. (1980) *The Popular Handbook of Rarer British Birds* (rev. edn.)

Owen, M. *et al.* (1986) *Wildfowl in Great Britain* (2nd edn.)

Perrins, C. (1987) *New Generation Guide to the Birds of Britain and Europe*

Prater, A. J. (1981) *Estuary Birds of Britain and Ireland*

Sharrock, J. T. R. (1976) *The Atlas of Breeding Birds in Britain and Ireland*

Thom, V. M. (1986) *Birds in Scotland*

Witherby, H. F. *et al.* (1940) *The Handbook of British Birds*

Also the magazines *Birds* and *Bird Notes* (of the RSPB), *Bird Study* (of the BTO) and *British Birds*.

Acknowledgements

I would like to thank all those who, in my younger years as a birdwatcher, provided so much essential advice and help. People like the late Professor Brian Collinge, Professor Bill Hale, the late Dr Jeffery Harrison, David Hindle, Maurice Jones, Len Knowles, the late Norman Harwood, Andrew Lassey, Harry Shorrock, Ken Spencer, Philip Thompson, the late Kenneth Williamson and my brother Philip. I would also mention the late James Fisher, Maxwell Knight and Sir Peter Scott who, by their writings, radio and television programmes and a few kindly words, encouraged the development of a keen young naturalist in the 1950s and early 1960s when wildlife, conservation and 'green' issues were of interest to only a very tiny minority. I would also thank the staff and members of the British Trust for Ornithology, the Royal Society for the Protection of Birds and the Wildfowl Trust.

The black and white illustrations were drawn by Terence Lambert, and the colour illustrations by Lyn Cawley, Graeme Chambers, Brin Edwards, Alexandra Head, Mike Iley, Ruth Lindsay, Kevin Marks, Michelle Ross, and Cathy Simpson. The maps are by Richard Geiger. The photographs in the introduction are my own.

Index